The HEDGE SCHOOLS
OF
IRELAND

P. J. Dowling

MERCIER PRESS

ACKNOWLEDGEMENTS

The author wishes to express his thanks to Mr. Padraic Colum for permission to quote his poem, *A Poor Scholar of the Forties,* to the Clarendon Press, Oxford, for permission to quote two passages from *Robin Flower: The Irish Tradition,* and to Messrs. Constable & Co. Ltd. for permission to quote one passage from *Helen Waddell: The Wandering Scholars.*

His thanks are also due to The Sign of the Three Candles, Dublin and to the Stationery Office, Dublin for permission to quote short passages from *Eleanor Knott: Irish Classical Poetry* and *Seven Centuries of Irish Learning,* respectively.

He desires, also, to acknowledge certain obligations to the Director, The National Library, Dublin, to Mr. George Lodge and to Mr. Eamon O'Tuathail.

P. J. D.

London 1968

Contents

MERCIER PRESS
PO Box 5, 5 French Church Street, Cork
16 Hume Street, Dublin 2

© P. J. Dowling 1968

First published by Longmans, Green in 1935. This edition first published in 1968.

ISBN 1 85635 181 5

*Trade enquiries to CMD DISTRIBUTION,
55a Spruce Avenue, Stillorgan Industrial Park, Blackrock, Dublin*

14 13 12 11 10 9 8 7 6 5 4

Printed in Ireland by Colour Books Ltd.

CHAPTER I

The Disappearance of the Old Order

The Hedge Schools enter upon the stage but a brief period after the exit of the Bardic Schools, the ancient professional schools of Ireland. According to a statement prefacing the Clanrickarde Memoirs, the Bardic Schools survived 'till the Beginnings of the Trouble in 1641'; these 'truly National Schools,' as O'Curry called them, closed down for good only when their patrons had become landless and homeless, or exiles.

It was not the fall of the Bardic Schools that brought the Hedge Schools into being. The Hedge Schools owe their origin to the suppression of all the ordinary legitimate means of education, first during the Cromwellian *regime* and then under the Penal Code introduced in the reign of William III and operating from that time in increasing measure till 1782. The Bardic Schools on the other hand, had represented a highly developed system providing, up to nearly the middle of the seventeenth century, the nearest approach to what might be called a university education; and as such could have nothing in common with the Hedge Schools as regards either content or method of education. It may have happened, however, that the disbanded students of the Bardic Schools took up teaching either in the interests of learning or through economic necessity. But there is no evidence of this, though in the lean years that followed few other occupations were open to them.

II

The Bardic Schools were purely secular institutions. The medium of instruction was the native tongue; and the Irish language and literature, Irish history, and the Brehon law were intensively and scientifically studied. For centuries they produced a long succession of poets, historians and brehons. The gifts of poet and chronicler were often united in the same person and occasionally the brehon was also a poet. The earliest account in English that we seem to have of them comes from the pen of Thomas Smyth, a Dublin apothecary, writing in 1561: 'Their is in Ireland four shepts in Maner all Rimers. The firste of them is calleid the Brehounde, which in English is calleid the Judge... The seconde sourte is the Shankee which is to saye in English the Petigrer... The thirde sorte is calleid the Aeosdan, which is to saye in English, the bards, or the rimine sepetes... The fourth sort of Rymers is calleid Fillis, which is to saye in English a Poete.'[1] The distinction between the *bard* and the *file* appears to be quite marked: 'the *bard* was simply a poet and versifier; the *file* a poet, but also a scholar and guardian of traditional knowledge.'[2] However, owing to the common use of the term, *bard,* to cover not only the rhymer and poet but also the chronicler and lawyer, we shall employ the terms, *bardic school* and *bard,* in these pages – with due apologies.

The best description we have of a Bardic School at work is given in the Preface to the Clanrickarde Memoirs, published in London in 1722. It was a school of poetry, and open only to students who were themselves descendants of poets and already of some distinction in their tribes. The school was situated in a quiet spot away from the families and friends of the students so that their studies should suffer no interruption. The school building was a simple construction with no windows, and furnished with a table, couch and chair for each student, who had a cubicle of his own. On the evening of the first day, the students were given a subject on which to write a poem; then they withdrew to their cubicles to compose their poems in complete darkness. There they remained till next evening when candles were brought and they wrote down their compositions. These were given to their professors in the assembly hall and examined by them. On Saturdays and the eves of Feasts, the students were entertained by the gentlemen and rich farmers of the neighbourhood. The school was open from Michaelmas to the 25th March, when the students returned to their homes, each one carrying with him an important document, namely, 'an Attestation of his Behaviour and Capacity, from the chief Professor, to those that had sent him.'[3] The period of training was a long one, 'six or seven years before a Mastery, or the last Degree was conferr'd.' Professor David Greene points out that there is no direct evidence that the period of training took seven years, or that the students composed their poems in a dormitory without lights 'but,' he adds, 'the remarkable amount of teaching material which has come down to us... shows that there must have been a severe academic discipline.'[4]

The Bardic Schools seem to have been of a strictly exclusive character; professors and students were confined to certain tribes and families. The anonymous prefacer of the Clanrickarde Memoirs, who has been identified by Robin Flower as Thomas O'Sullivan, a Tipperary man, tells us that 'the Brehons (Judges) be of one Stock and Name, the Historians of another; and so of the rest who instruct their own Children and Kinsmen, and have some of them always to be their Successors.' Osborn Bergin confesses that he has never come upon a description in Irish of a Bardic School. He says, however, that the professional classes in Ireland were so conservative that Clanrickarde's description was undoubtedly accurate.[5]

St. Patrick's mission to Ireland and the conversion of the Irish people to Christianity do not appear to have affected the Bardic Schools either in importance or in numbers, except, of course, that they no longer trained druids. Robin Flower suggests that 'the relations between monastic men of letters and the poets must have been close: and they were sometimes uneasy.'[6] The study of Latin seems to have been taken up in the Bardic Schools at an early date. O'Curry vouches for the classical knowledge of the poets of the tenth and eleventh centuries, and Quiggin for the familiarity of poets of the thirteenth, fourteenth, and fifteenth centuries 'with religious literature in the Latin language.'[7] Edmund Campion has given us a description of a medical school where the students spoke 'Latine like a vulgar language.' But according to the Rev. Francis Shaw: 'The notion that at the end of the sixteenth century Latin was the language of the Irish medical schools is irreconcilable with the evidence of the Irish manuscripts.'[8]

Ireland under the Tudors witnessed a decline in the Bardic Schools. The wars of Henry VIII and Elizabeth I reduced the power and the fortunes of many Irish chiefs and Anglo-norman lords who were patrons of the schools. The bards themselves, by keeping alive the spirit of nationality, were a direct menace to English rule in Ireland; and as a result of their activities they often suffered considerable hardship. For instance, in 1563 the Earl of Desmond had to give an undertaking that no bard would be allowed to reside within the counties of Cork, Limerick and Kerry.[9] The poet Spenser disapproved of them, also. He, no doubt, was afraid that the bard might at any time arouse the resentment of those who had been dispossessed of the lands he occupied. He had some of the bardic poems translated for him; and he gives them a sort of grudging admiration.

Before the end of the first decade of the seventeenth century, the whole country was completely under English domination; very many estates had been confiscated to the Crown; and the great northern chiefs, the patrons of the Bardic Schools of Ulster, had fled to the Continent. But it was Cromwell's destructive campaign, and the redistribution of land, and the plantation of large territories then and later which brought about the closing of the schools.

But after the Commonwealth period, there were still

families which retained, somehow or other, the services of the bard. 'The nobility and gentry,' wrote Sir Henry Piers in 1682, 'value themselves very high on the stock of their antiquity and descent, and in this respect they little set by others; you shall meet with one or more antiquaries, as they are termed, that is deducers of their pedigrees, in every great family.'[10]

But at the beginning of the eighteenth century, the state of native learning must have been at its lowest ebb. An extract from the preface to the Clanrickarde Memoirs would seem to make this clear: 'The Study of the present Generation reaching no farther than to comprehend and write the common Dialect of the Language... Nor could it have been well otherwise, where not so much as one Country School of that kind hath been frequented since the Beginning of the Wars of 1641; the Gentlemen, and Quality, for the most part, that countenanc'd and supported that sort of Learning, having been thrust out of their Estates.'

The schools are said to have declined into 'Courts of Poetry', assemblies at which poetry was recited and discussed.[11] A distinguished London doctor, who spent several years in Ireland prior to 1767, gives an account of literary gatherings at which he was present: 'In *Ireland* they have their bards to this day, among the inland inhabitants; and even among the poorest of the people;... and it is a very common practice among them when they return home from the toil of the day, to sit down, with their people around them, in bad weather, in their houses, and without doors in fair, repeating the histories of ancient heroes and their transactions, in a stile that, for its beauty, and fine sentiments has often struck me with amazement.'[12] He does not say, unfortunately, in which parts of the country these meetings took place. The Protestant Rector of Dungiven, County Derry, writing about the year 1814, makes this interesting statement: 'The manner of preserving the accuracy of tradition is singular, and worthy of notice. In the winter evenings, a number of seanachies frequently meet together, and recite alternately their traditionary stories. If anyone repeats a passage, which appears to another to be incorrect, he is immediately stopped, when each gives a reason for his way of reciting the passage, the dispute is then referred to a vote of the meeting, and the decision of the majority becomes imperative on the subject for the future.'[13]

Professor Tomas O'Maille tells us that he took down a version of Donnchadh Mór O'Dalaigh's famous poem from the lips of a seanchaidhe of County Galway. The poem, consisting of fifty-five stanzas, each of four lines, was composed about the early thirteenth century. A remarkable instance of the faithfulness with which Irish literature has been transmitted to us, down the years.[14]

Robin Flower relates that when on a visit to one of the Blasket Islands he met a man of over eighty years of age who recited for him long poems, and ancient Irish tales. 'I listened spellbound,' he says, 'and, as I listened, it came to me suddenly that there on the last inhabited piece of European land, looking out to the Atlantic horizon, I was hearing the oldest living tradition in the British Isles... So far as the record goes this matter in one form or another is older than the Anglo-Saxon Beowulf, and yet it lives still upon the lips of the peasantry, a real and vivid experience, while, except to a few painful scholars, Beowulf has long passed out of memory. To-morrow this too will be dead, and the world will be the poorer when this last shade of that which once was great has passed away.'[15]

III

The Bardic Schools, as we have said, had lasted, in fading glory, till almost the middle of the seventeenth century. While still pagan, they saw the coming of Christianity; first, through the traders from Rome and other places on the Continent; then through the contact of Ireland with Wales, for long a Roman province; and, finally, through the missionary work of St. Patrick. In time, Ireland became wholly Christian. There had been monks in Ireland before St. Patrick's arrival; but only in a few scattered communities.

The history of the Monastic schools of Ireland begins with the School of Armagh, founded by St. Patrick himself, about A. D. 450. The School of St. Enda in Aranmore was also a fifth century foundation; so were fourteen others, including the stern School of St. Brigid. In the sixth and seventh centuries some thirty schools were founded.

As early as the sixth century, the Irish Monastic Schools attracted great numbers of students from Western Europe and from Britain. In A. D. 550, fifty students from the Loire district of France disembarked at Cork.[16] The Venerable Bede, writing, more than a century later, of his own countrymen who went to Ireland, says: 'The Scots received them all, and took care to supply them with food, as also to furnish them with books to read, and their teaching, gratis.'[17]

But even while students were coming to Ireland from abroad, Irish monks were leaving their own country to preach the Gospel in places where it was still unknown. As Helen Waddell said: 'That fierce and restless quality which had made the pagan Irish the terror of Western Europe, seems to have emptied itself into the love of learning and the love of God; and it is the peculiar distinction of Irish mediaeval scholarship and the salvation of literature in Europe that the one in no way conflicted with the other.'[18] Ciaran of Saighir sojourned in several places in Britain and taught the people there; Columcille became the apostle of Scotland; Columbanus and his disciples founded more than a hundred monasteries in France, Germany, Switzerland and Italy; and so the story goes on for four or five centuries after the time of Columbanus.

The invasion of the Danes towards the end of the eighth century arrested the development of Irish monasticism. The monasteries were pillaged and burnt to the ground, the monks were killed or put to flight, their sacred vessels and manuscripts were seized or destroyed. But the missionary zeal of the monks was undiminished; even more of them went abroad; a few brought with them some of their treasures saved from the hands of the barbarians. It has been estimated that there are only about ten Irish manuscripts of date before A. D. 1000 in Ireland, whereas there are over fifty on the Continent.[19]

Two hundred years of Danish domination took a heavy toll of learning in Ireland and of its reputation for holiness and austerity of life. But there were still monks who shed glory on their country; men like Virgilius the Geometer, Sedulius of Liege, the great John Scotus Eriugena, *and* others, remarkable alike for their devotion to duty as for their learning. And all of them received their training in Irish monasteries.

Not long after the death of Columbanus, the monasteries he founded adopted the less severe Rule of St. Benedict. At home, the Rule was not, or could not have been, strictly kept owing to the continual ravages of the Northmen and, later, the quarrels between the rival claimants for the High Kingship of Ireland. There was an attempt to revive the Rule of Columbanus in the eleventh century; but this was delayed owing to the unsettled state of the country, and finally ended by the Norman invasion.

But, shortly before this, the first Cistercian house, the Abbey of Mellifont, was founded; and so much did the Cistercian way of life appeal to the ascetic side of the Irish character that within twelve years there were no less than ten Cistercian monasteries in Ireland. The Canons Regular of St. Augustine were also here before the coming of the Normans, and by the end of the twelfth century they had founded about fifteen priories.

Though most of the religious houses in the twelfth and thirteenth centuries were Norman foundations, it is worthy of note that twenty-eight of the thirty-nine Cistercian houses were Irish foundations. The Dominicans came in 1224, the Franciscans in 1230 or a little earlier, and the Carmelites in 1274.

Irish students entered the new monasteries in such numbers that in 1310 a Parliament at Kilkenny passed a law forbidding religious orders within the Pale to accept anyone who was not English. Eleven years later, it was decreed that no monastery should refuse to admit an Englishman. While a statute of 1380 again expressly forbade monasteries to receive Irishmen.

In 1537, Henry VIII was declared by Act of Parliament Supreme Head of the Church in Ireland; and in 1539, the suppression of the monasteries began. Foundations, centuries old, saw the monks expelled and their possessions taken away. The buildings which had been the pride of the pious founders came into the hands of the despoiler, and were pulled down or suffered to fall into decay. Not one of them has been rebuilt.

The question has often been raised as to whether the later medieval monasteries and convents made provision for the education of boys and girls other than those intended for the religious life. There is a suggestion that this was so in a letter, dated 21 May 1539, written by Lord Leonard Gray, then Lord Deputy of Ireland, to Thomas Cromwell, King Henry VIII's Chancellor, begging that six of the monasteries within the Pale should be spared the fate of the rest: 'Saint Marie Abbay adjoynying to Dublin, a House of White Monkes; Christes Churche, a house of Chanons, situate in the middle of the citie of Dublin; the Nunrie of Grace-Dewe in the countie of Dublin; Connall in the countie of Kildare; Kenlys and Gerepont, in the countie of Kilkenny.' For in these, he points out, 'yonge men and childer, bothe gentilmen childer and other, bothe of man kynd and women kynd, be broght up in vertue, lernyng, and in the English tonge and behavior, to the grete charges of the said houses; that is to say, the women kynd of the hole Englishrie of this land, for the more part, in the said Nunnrie, and the man kynd in the other said houses.'[20] His appeal fell on deaf ears and the monasteries were closed. Later, we are told, he took a substantial share himself of the plunder of the religious houses.

One result of Henry VIII's policy was the establishment in certain cities of schools for the education, chiefly, of the children of the Anglo-Norman settlers. In 1565, Father Peter White, Fellow of Oriel College, Oxford, taught a school at Kilkenny, founded by the Earl of Ormond, of which Richard Stanyhurst, one of his pupils gives an interesting account. He acknowledges his indebtedness to his master: 'And bicause it was my happie hap (God and my parents be thanked) to haue beene one of his crue, I take it to stand with my dutie, sith I may not stretch mine abilitie in requiting his good turnes, yet to manifest my good will in remembering his paines. And certes, I acknowledge my selfe so much bounde and beholding to him and his, as for his sake I reuerence the meanest stone cemented in the wals of that famous schoole.'[21]

Many years later, Robert Payne came upon what may have been a similar type of school in Limerick. 'I saw in a Grammer schoole in *Limbrick,*' he says, 'one hundred & threscore schollers, most of them speaking good and perfit English, for that they haue vsed to conster the Latin into English.'[22]

We learn that Waterford possessed more than one school about the same time, 1585 or thereabouts, from a letter written by a Protestant schoolmaster complaining to the Lord Primate of Ireland that his pupils were being taken away from him and sent to a Catholic school in the city: 'The reason they allege why they took them away was, because, as they say, for that they did not profit; for I constrained them to come to the ser-

16

vice, which they could not abide, whereat they mu
privately among themselves.'[23]

Outside the Pale, in places where English rule aid ...
extend to the fullness of its power, some monasteries
appear to have escaped the general destruction. Sir
John Davies, Attorney-General of Ireland, writing to the
Earl of Salisbury in 1607, points out that 'the Abbies
and Religious houses in *Tyrone, Tirconnell,* and *Fer-
managh,* though they were dissolved in the 33rd of Henry
8th, were never surveyed nor reduced into charge,
but were continually possest by the religious persons,
until His Majesty, that now is, came to the Crown.'[24]

Though there is this evidence of the existence of Irish
monasteries at the end of the sixteenth century, it is
significant that between the years 1582 and 1681 about
twenty colleges for Irish Catholic students were founded
on the Continent: Salamanca in 1582, Lisbon in 1595,
Douai in 1596, Antwerp in 1600, Toulouse in 1660,
Paris in 1677. One was founded at Prague in 1631; and
there were at least four foundations in Rome, established
in 1625, 1626, 1656 and 1677 respectively. Testimony that
opportunities of higher education at home were becoming increasingly difficult, and that there were few
or no facilities for the education of those intended for
the Church.

These colleges received great numbers of young men
who left Ireland to study for the priesthood, for the
army, for medicine and for law, and in their turn made
necessary the continued existence of schools in Ireland
for the education of future entrants. No doubt, many
students had had their earlier education in foreign
schools; but it is also certain that most of the students
received their early training at home. In an official
document, thought to be written about 1618, there is a
reference to the number of students in these colleges:
'There are hundredes in the Colledges whose names I
sawe the last lent from Waterford, Limerick, Clon-
mell, Corck, Gallway, Kilkenny, and Drogheda, and

from the counteyes abroad throughout the realme and I
am sure yt there is noe worthy gent in all the realme,
nor merchaunt but have there somme of theire neerest
kinsemen but what in the particuller is sent unto them
is the porcon there fathers doe leave them, and some
collections that yearely is taken upp for them, and wth.
this they live togeather wth. certaine yearely pen-
sions that is allowed unto the colledges by ye Kinges
and Princes in whose dominions they are.'[25]

The records of the Irish College, Salamanca, give
valuable information about each student: his name, the
names of his parents, the diocese he came from, and the
names of his teachers. For example, in the declaration,
on oath, of Theobald Jennings on entering the college,
in 1620, it is stated (in Latin) that he was born in the
county of Mayo in the diocese of Tuam, and from an
early date studied the Humanities under Isaac Mullaly
and Alexander Lynch.[26]

This Alexander Lynch was probably the schoolmaster
compelled to give up teaching by the Royal Commission
appointed by James I to inquire into the state of the
Irish dioceses. The Commissioners reported: 'Wee
found in Galway a publique schoolesmaster named
Lynch, placed there by the Cittizens, who had great
numbers of Schollers, not only out of that province but
also out of the Pale, and other partes resorting to him.
Wee had daily proofe, during our continuance in that
citty, how well his schollers profited under him, by
versions and orations which they presented us. Wee sent
for that schoolemaster before us, and seriously advised
him to conform to the Religion established, and not pre-
vailing with our advices, we enjoyned him to forbear
teaching.'[27]

Though the suppression of schools in the first half of
the sixteenth century was of frequent occurrence, yet
there was much educational activity on the part of religious orders, notably the Dominicans, Franciscans and
Jesuits, both then and later.

18

Even under the Commonwealth, education was somehow continued though the penalties for daring to teach were very great indeed. Among references to schoolmasters in the Commonwealth Records we find entries like this: 'Order touching popish-Schoolmasters to be transplanted into Connaught. The Councel take into consideration, that such persons corrupt the youth of this Nation with Popish principals. Such schoolmasters to bee secured, and put on board of such ship bound for the Islands of the Barbadoes.'[28]

The reign of Charles II, following one of the harshest periods in the history of Ireland, seems to have been, in spite of the strictures on Catholic worship, a time of comparative security for the Irish Catholic. We learn, too, that opportunities of education were greater. A contemporary writer, Sir Henry Piers, whom we have already quoted in another context, is witness to this: 'The people still retain an ardent desire for learning,' he said, 'and both at home and abroad do attain unto good measures thereof. There are from the highest to the lowest classes of them that are very ingenious and docile; in this only unhappy, that they will not breed their youth in our universities, neither in this kingdom nor in England, because of the religion therein professed, but choose rather, being not permitted to have public schools of their own, to educate their children under private professors, or else send them abroad into France or Spain for their breeding.'[29] Indeed, the growth of Catholic schools was a source of serious disturbance to Erasmus Smith, who complained in that very year, 1682, that the schools of which he was founder and benefactor were suffering because of the popularity of the Catholic schools in their immediate vicinity.. 'My Lords... my designe is not to reflect upon any,' he wrote to the Governors of his schools, 'only I give my Judgement why these schooles are so consumptive, which was, and is, and will be (if not prevented) the many popish schooles, theire neighbours, which as succers doo starve the tree.'[30]

Education may be said to have flourished during the brief reign of James II but only insofar as teachers and buildings were available. For the first time in the history of Ireland, a Catholic was appointed Provost of Trinity College, Dublin and for the first time a Catholic university was founded in Ireland; not in Dublin but in Kilkenny city which was within reach of most of the principal towns in the south of Ireland and far enough away from Dublin not to draw students from that city or from the counties north and west of Dublin.

But with the accession of William III to the throne and the introduction of the Penal Laws by an Irish government in this and subsequent reigns, the promise of the previous years went for nothing.

NOTES

1. Ulster Journal of Archaeology. Vol. 6. 1868.
2. Eleanor Knott; Irish Classical Poetry, p. 7.; See also David Greene: Seven Centuries of Irish Learning. pp. 46, 50.
3. Clanrickarde Memoirs. pp. clviii-clxi.
4. Seven Centuries of Irish Learning. p. 51.
5. Journal of the Ivernian Society. Vol. V. pp. 155–56.
6. The Irish Tradition, p. 75.
7. Manners and Customs. II. p. 104. Prologomena. p. 32.
8. Seven Centuries of Irish Learning. p. 96.
9. Calendar of Patent Rolls. I. pp. 486–7.
10. Choreographical Description of the County of Meath. p. 109.
11. Corkery: The Hidden Ireland. Chap. IV. and Kenney: Sources for the Early History of Ireland. p. 53 et seq.
12. Parsons: Remains of Japhet. p. 148.
13. Mason: Parochial Survey. Vol. I. p. 318.
14. Archivium Hibernicum. Vol. II. p. 256.
15. The Irish Tradition, p. 105.
16. Waddell: The Wandering Scholars, p. 29.
17. Ecclesiastical History of England. 1894. p. 163.
18. The Wandering Scholars. p. 28.
19. Kenney: Sources. p. 9.

20. State Papers, Henry VIII. Ed. Brewer. Vol. III. pp. 130–1.
21. Description of Ireland, written in 1568. London 1808 p. 34.
22. A Brife Description of Ireland, 1589. p. 3.
23. See Calendar of State Papers, 1574–85. p. 573.
24. A Discovery of the True Causes why Ireland was never sub-dued. p. 53.
25. The MS. is preserved in Trinity College, Dublin. E. 3. 15.
26. Archivium Hibernicum. Vol. III. p. 93.
27. Given in O'Flaherty: Description of West Connaught. p. 215.
28. Printed in Archivium Hibernicum. Vol. VI. pp. 188–9.
29. Choreographical Description of the County of Meath, p. 112.
30. PP. 1857–8. XXII. Part I. p. 23.

CHAPTER II

Education and the Penal Code

'The legislation on the subject of Catholic education,'
wrote Lecky, the Protestant historian, 'may be briefly
described, for it amounted simply to universal, unqualified, and unlimited proscription.' It has been said more
than once that the laws against education were never
put rigorously into force; but there is much evidence to
the contrary. The obstacles in the way of education both
at home and abroad were very real indeed. Schoolmasters were imprisoned and fined. Substantial re-
wards were offered and given to those who brought
about their conviction. Magistrates were empowered to
examine on oath any person over the age of sixteen, and
anyone who was suspected of knowing that schools
were being taught in the neighbourhood, or that young
people had been sent abroad for their education was,
therefore, obliged to tell what he knew. Protestant
schoolmasters were forbidden to employ Catholics as
assistant teachers; and magistrates were warned to
attend strictly both to the letter *and* to the spirit of the
law. Schoolmaster, householder, and friendly magistrate
were equally good game for the informer.

Things may have eased a little from time to time, but
there were always people in authority seeking to continue the suppression of education. In 1740, Sir Richard
Cox, in his charge to the Grand Jury of Cork, urged the
jurors, the actual administrators of justice, to take upon
themselves the rôle of prosecutors of the law in order to
hasten the conviction of offending schoolmasters: 'You
are not to wait for regular Information;' he said, 'if the
Offendors are within your Knowledge, you may and
ought to present them.' And as late as December, 1760,
we learn that the authorities still viewed foreign education with extreme disfavour. In his address to the Grand

Juries of Dublin City and County, Judge Robinson gave this direction: 'You are to Enquire of, and Present, all Misprisons of Treason, all Offences against the Acts of Parliament, made in this Kingdom, to restrain the Education of our Youth in Foreigh Popish Seminaries; to hinder Papists bearing Arms at Home; and to prevent the King's Subjects from Enlisting in Foreign Service, without his Majesty's Licence; and all Offences against the Statute of Premunire.'

This Act of William III, 'An Act to Restrain Foreign Education', was clearly intended to put an end to Catholic education. It was of this Act that Edmund Burke wrote: 'While this restraint upon foreign and domestic education was part of a horrible and impious system of servitude, the members were well fitted to the body. To render men patient under a deprivation of all the rights of human nature, everything which could give them a knowledge or feeling of these rights was rationally forbidden. To render humanity to be insulted, it was fit that it should be degraded.'

Promise of relief came with the Act of 1782. This Act admitted the undue severity of the laws against education and their failure in the object for which they were intended; wherefore the Acts of William and Anne which forbade 'persons of the popish religion' to teach were now repealed.

This was not a charter of liberty to teach. The schoolmaster was free to teach, but only on certain conditions. He had to take the oath of allegiance to the Crown. He could not have Protestant children in his school. He was not allowed to teach in a Protestant school – we have instances, however, of Catholic teachers being 'entertained to instruct youth in learning, as usher, under-master, or assistant' by Protestant schoolmasters: Patrick Lynch, for example, taught in the Rev. Mr. Hare's school at Cashel; and Dr. Lanigan, afterwards Bishop of Ossory, had held the post of usher in a Protestant school at Carrick-on-Suir owned by the Rev.

23

Mr. Jackson, and before that he had been a pupil at the same school – all of which was contrary to the law. But no legal action appears to have been taken against them. The harshest condition imposed by the Act of 1782 was that no 'popish university or college' could be erected or endowed, and that no school could be endowed. This is generally regarded as a new penal law against education. Lastly, before a teacher could set up his school the Act required him to obtain a licence to teach from the Protestant bishop of the diocese or his representative who was empowered to grant such a licence, and to withdraw it at will.

Hope of further relief came with the Act of 1792 which declared that a licence to teach was no longer necessary, provided that the person who wished to 'teach or keep school' should 'in all other respects... conform himself' to the Act of 1782. But there is ample evidence to show that licences were applied for and granted after 1792. The licences granted to the Presentation Convent, Waterford, and the Ursuline Convent, Thurles, are both dated 1799; the licence given to the Presentation Convent, Kilkenny, is dated 1801; while that obtained by the Rev. Garret Connolly on behalf of St. John's College, Waterford, is, dated 1819. The licence given to one of them will help to explain the procedure by which a licence was obtained; the licence granted to the Presentation Convent Kilkenny, reads as follows: 'By the tenor of these presents, We, Hugh, by Divine permission Lord Bishop of Ossory, send Greetings to Isabella McLoughlin of the parish of St. Mary, in our said Diocese. Whereas you are sufficiently recommended unto us as a proper person to keep school within our said Diocese for the education and instruction of Papists or persons professing the Popish Religion. We do therefore by these presents give and grant unto you full leave and Licence to keep and teach a school within the said parish during our Will and pleasure only, for the Education and Instruction of Children of Popish Parents only, you having first produced to us a certificate of your having taken the Oath of allegiance and declaration prescribed to be taken by law. In testimony whereof We have caused the seal of our Constitutional Court of Ossory to be hereunto affixed the twenty-fifth of May. In the year of our Lord one thousand eight hundred and one. (Seal) Paul Helsham, Vicar-General.'

The recommendation as to the character of the applicant for a licence to teach had to be obtained from the local Protestant clergyman; and if this were not procured no licence would be granted. When the Rev. Peter Kenny, S.J. sought for a licence to teach in the year 1814, the Parish Minister of Clane refused to give him the necessary recommendation. On appealing to the Rev. Rawdon Greene, Registrar of the Diocese of Kildare, he was told 'Mr. Greene is concerned that he is obliged to inform Mr. Kenny that the License cannot possibly be granted without such Certificate.'

It is extremely doubtful if hedge schoolmasters, or indeed if any, except a few, lay teachers sought licences to teach. The safety of the schoolmaster was in his obscurity. There was no certainty that the best qualified applicant would obtain a licence; and there was no guarantee that having obtained it he would be allowed to continue to hold it. So it was that the Hedge Schools, often described by contemporary writers as 'unlicensed schools', were illegal schools till the passing of the Catholic Emancipation Act in 1829.

CHAPTER III

English schools in Ireland on Public and Private Foundation before 1782

The earliest schools established in Ireland by Act of Parliament were the Parish Schools of Henry VIII, the purpose of which was to introduce a knowledge of the English language among the native Irish. This Act enjoined on oath every clergyman to 'keepe, or cause to be kept, within the place, territory, or paroch, where he shall have... benefice or promotion, a schole for to learne English.' The clergyman was directed to 'bid the beades in the Englishe tongue, and preach the word of God in English.'

In 1570, during the reign of Elizabeth I, a second Act of Parliament was passed; this time for the establishment of 'a free schoole within every diocesse' in Ireland. 'The Schoolemaster' was to be 'an Englishman, or of the English birth of this realm;' and his school was intended to provide education of a grammar school kind.

In the reign of Charles I, the Free Schools of Royal Foundation, originally endowed by James I, came into being. These were also grammar schools. There was still a third group of grammar schools, known as Classical Schools of Private Foundation, established, as their name implies, out of funds bequeathed for that purpose by private individuals.

There also appeared in Ireland a number of schools, officially called English Schools of Private Foundation. They were about sixty-five in number; and were chiefly set up in the eighteenth century for the elementary education of Protestant children in poor circumstances. They were known as English Schools because it was not intended to teach Latin in them.

In 1669, three free grammar schools were founded under a royal charter by a London merchant, named Erasmus Smith, from the revenues of certain lands confiscated to the Crown after the Rising of 1641 and purchased by him under the Commonwealth settlement at a modest figure. The value of the foundation increased so much during the eighteenth century that at the beginning of the nineteenth the name of Erasmus Smith was associated with grants to Trinity College, Dublin, and to a number of schools, and with the foundation of a fourth grammar school and of well over a hundred 'English' schools.

These schools do not seem to have affected the education of the people as a whole, partly because of their limited numbers and partly because of the increasing number of schools of native growth. The Reports of the Board of Education, 1808-1812, stated that the Parish and Diocesan Schools were a failure. The Royal Schools did not seem to have fared much better. The Classical Schools of Private Foundation were found to be nearly all pay-schools, though many of them were intended to be free schools and all of them were expected to admit free scholars. Only the English Schools of Private Foundation appeared to have respected the expressed wishes of their founders, for, as far as one can judge, they encountered less difficulties, financial and administrative, than other groups of schools; they were more generous in the matter of free scholars; and, in general, they were more tolerant in the matter of religion. The Erasmus Smith schools did not come under investigation by the Commissioners of the Board of Education in 1808 as the other schools did; for, according to the terms of the charter, their schools could not be entered except by the express permission of the trustees or by Act of Parliament.

The last group of schools founded before 1782 were the Charter Schools. In a letter to the bishop of London, dated May 5 1730, Archbishop Boulter wrote: 'The great number of papists in this kingdom, and the obstinacy with which they adhere to their own religion, occasions our trying what may be done with their children to bring them over to our church.'[1] The only children that could be obtained for this purpose would naturally be the children of the very poor who would yield them up to save them from starvation. A petition to George II over the signatures of 'the principal Nobility, Clergy and Gentry of Ireland' brought them a charter to set up 'a sufficient number of English Protestant Schools... as one of the most effectual means of Converting and civilising the Irish natives.' Money was soon forthcoming for the project; and within a few years some fifty-eight schools were built. Indeed, it is estimated that between the year 1733, when the charter was granted, and the year 1824, when parliamentary grants were gradually withdrawn, the sum derived from public funds amounted to more than a million pounds and that obtained from private sources was little short of £600,000.

The schools were administered from Dublin by the Incorporated Society, formed to implement the charter, assisted by committees in various parts of the country which were supposed to exercise some supervision over the schools in their respective localities. But in practice the conduct of the schools was left entirely in the hands of the teachers, who were paid a salary of £12 a year and an allowance of £9 a year for feeding and clothing each child, as well as practically all the profit of the child's labour in the factory, or on the farm attached to each school. This financial arrangement led to enormous abuses: the children were overworked, badly fed and ill-clothed and in many cases were given no instruction at all. The children were at the mercy of their teachers, neglected alike by the local committees and by the Incorporated Society itself.

Visitors to the schools seem in general to have found them in an unsatisfactory condition. In 1773, John Wesley visited the Charter School at Ballinrobe; he described it as 'a picture of slothfulness, nastiness, and desolation;' he saw neither master nor mistress; nor a child, boy or girl, decently clothed. Some years later, John Howard visited a number of Charter Schools and from what he learnt as to the treatment and education of the children he was convinced that they needed 'a thorough parliamentary inquiry.' He said he found the children in the Hedge Schools 'much forwarder than those of the same age in the charter schools,' as well being 'clean and wholesome.'

The record of Sir Jeremiah Fitzpatrick's visit to the Charter School at Charleville on 2nd January, 1786, makes painful reading: 'When I arrived at this Place the Wether was exceedingly cold, and the Snow above twenty Inches deep. There were Seventeen Boys and Nine Girls in the School, all ragged. I entered the House unexpectedly, leaving my Servant at a Distance, which is my Custom, lest the idea of Inspection should occur to the Master. This Precaution afforded me the Opportunity of seeing two little Girls sitting on a table in the School-room, which was damp and clay-floored, without any Fire; their little legs were under each other's Petticoats to keep them warm; at the same Time a Girl of ten Years old was blowing on her Infant Sister's fingers to procure them a temporary Relief from the excessive Cold. The Windows of every Room were broken, the Beds filthy; and there was not a single Sheet in the House for the Childrens Use, whose Education was shamefully neglected.'[2]

During the next forty years, the abuses seem to have continued almost without intermission. Englishmen like Wakefield and Steven exposed the Charter Schools and condemned them, while Irishmen like Richard Lovell Edgeworth and Elias Thackery were completely blind to the harm they wrought. The Report of the Board of Education, 1808-12, stated that they had failed to achieve the object of their establishment, namely, 'the conversion of the lower orders of the Inhabitants of Ireland from the errors of Popery.'[3] According to Froude, they were 'a conspicuous and a monstrous failure.'[4] After 1830, the parliamentary grant was finally stopped.

The schools on public and private foundation did not make any great impact upon the education of the people as a whole. Their work was clearly confined to a minority. Most of them, even those which made a bad start in their early years, emerged towards the middle of the nineteenth century with assured status. They had recovered from the changes of circumstance and fortune through which they had passed.

NOTES

1. Letters. Vol. II. p. 10.
2. House of Commons Journal Vol. XII. Pt. II p.dcccxxi.
3. P.P. 1813–14. V. p. 24. See also P.P. 1825. XII. p. 29.
4. 'The English in Ireland'. Vol. II. p. 450.

CHAPTER IV

The Education Societies

The restriction that it was still illegal after 1782 to endow schools, hampered effectively the development of Catholic education. Consequently, free education among Catholics was not common. But it did not prevent the spread and increase of schools set up by private individuals in town and country. John Leslie Foster, in a letter to the Secretary of the Board of Education in 1811, stated that 'Hardly any other country' was 'so amply provided with the means of education.' He warned the Board that the people were 'taking education into their own hands,' and that it was high time for the State to interfere.[1]

There was no clearly defined response on the part of the Government. But it lent its support, and in some instances granted large sums of money to certain societies which professed to undertake the education of the poor in Ireland. These were usually referred to as 'Bible Societies', because the Bible was the staple of instruction in all their schools.

A parliamentary grant of £300 was given in 1801 to the 'Association incorporated for Discountenancing Vice, and Promoting the Knowledge and Practice of the Christian Religion.' By 1823, the grant had increased to over £9,000. The schools of this body were admittedly Protestant in character; and nothing was taught in them contrary to the doctrines of the Established Church in Ireland.

The schools of the London Hibernian Society, founded in 1806, professed, on the other hand, to be undenominational, but certainly were not. The society received no parliamentary grant; instead, it obtained large sums of money from the Lord Lieutenant's Fund, thereby getting grants from public money voted annually for school buildings.

The Baptist Society, established in London in 1814, set up nearly three-fourths of its eighty-eight schools in the province of Connaught, none in Ulster, using the Irish language as the medium of instruction. Its activities were more in the nature of a religious mission than of an educational undertaking. 'The intention of proselytism,' wrote a contemporary, an Anglican clergyman, 'is everywhere avowed in the most unqualified manner.'[2]

The largest and most influential of these societies was the 'Society for promoting the Education of the Poor in Ireland,' usually called the Kildare Place Society from the location of its headquarters. It was instituted in 1811 with the object of rendering financial assistance to schools which gave an undertaking that the Scriptures would be read without note or comment, and that all books of a controversial nature would be excluded. In 1815, the Society was given a grant of £6,980 by Parliament with a view to putting into execution the recommendations of the Commissioners of the Board of Education, issued in 1812, to the effect that opportunities of education should be afforded to 'the lower classes of the People,' and that there should be no 'Interference with the particular Religious Tenets of any.'[3] The annual grant was later increased; and for several years before the Society was finally superseded in 1831 by the National Board of Education the amount of the grant was between twenty and thirty thousand pounds a year.

The educational work of the Kildare Place Society was on a wide and original scale.[4] They supplied plans for the construction of schools, they gave financial assistance towards the building and equipment of schools, they published school-books, they instituted a cheap library, they established a training college for teachers, and they organised a system of inspection of their schools. There is no doubt that the achievements of the Society were on a much higher level than that of any of its contemporaries but it seems to have been unable to resist the temptation of trying to proselytise the Catholic children in its schools. According to the Report of the Board of Education in 1825, it 'failed in producing universal Satisfaction.'[5] Sir Thomas Wyse, prominently identified with the advance of education in both England and Ireland, wrote in 1829: 'The Kildare Place Society, which set out with such large professions of liberalism, was demonstrated to have acted in a manner very inconsistent with the avowed objects of its institution, and to have been totally inadequate to the purposes for which it had originally been set up.'[6]

Members of the Church of Ireland objected to the schools assisted by the Society because the Bible was either read in the schools without note or comment, or was explained without any reference to authority. Catholics opposed them for somewhat similar reasons, but chiefly because they were employed as proselytising instruments – though for some years after its creation Catholics had ardently supported the Society.

In 1824, it was found that the number of schools financed, in whole or part, by the various societies was 1,727 out of a total number of 11,823. There were 9,352 pay-schools which received no assistance of any kind; and of these the Hedge Schools formed the majority. Thus the societies' schools, though in possession of substantial means and supported by Parliament, the public press and the landed gentry had not succeeded in establishing themselves as a popular system of education. The Commissioners of the Board of Education of 1824 plainly showed their lack of confidence in them by recommending, and eventually securing the establishment of a National Board of Education to be responsible for the administration of primary education in Ireland.

33

NOTES

1. P.P. 1813–14. V. p. 341 et seq.
2. Warburton: 'History of Dublin' Vol. II. p. 877.
3. P.P. 1813–14. V. p. 327.
4. Kingsmill Moore: 'An Unwritten Chapter...' p. 144.
5. P.P. 1825. XII. p. 58.
6. History of the Catholic Association. Vol. II. p. xcviii.

CHAPTER V

The Rise of the Hedge Schools

The beginnings of the Hedge School date back to the 17th century. The 'Popish Schoole Masrs.' mentioned in the Cromwellian Records who taught 'the Irish youth, trayning them up in Supersticion, Idolatry, and the Evil Customs of the Nacion'[1] were probably the first hedge schoolmasters.

But it was in the early part of the 18th century, when the continued rigorous enforcement of the laws against education rendered teaching a dangerous calling, that the Hedge School really took root. It was then, no doubt, that the term 'Hedge School' was first used.

Because the law forbade the schoolmaster to teach, he was compelled to give instruction secretly: because the householder was penalised for harbouring the schoolmaster, he had perforce to teach, and that only when the weather permitted, out of doors. He therefore, selected, in some remote spot, the sunny side of a hedge or bank which effectively hid him and his pupils from the eye of the chance passer-by, and there he sat upon a stone as he taught his little school, while his scholars lay stretched upon the green sward about him. One pupil was usually placed at a point of vantage to give warning of the approach of strangers; and if the latter were suspected of being law-officers or informers, the class was quickly disbanded for the day – only to meet again on the morrow in some place still more sheltered and remote.

In winter the schoolmaster moved from place to place living upon the hospitality of the people, earning a little perhaps by turning his hand to farm work, or, when he dared, by teaching the children of his host.

Later when the laws against education were less strictly enforced, school was taught in a cabin, a barn, or any building that might be given or lent for the purpose, but the name 'Hedge School' was still retained. The schoolhouses are generally referred to by contemporary writers as 'poor huts,' or 'cabbins.' Latocnaye, a Frenchman who walked through Ireland in 1797, carrying an umbrella and a pair of dancing pumps, tells us that the people are too poor to build a decent school house for their children, they can only afford to put up a wretched building, without windows, the roof of which is only about five feet high, extremely uncomfortable for both teachers and pupils. But when the weather permits the classes are held outside under a tree, or in the shelter of a hedge. This writer appreciates the advantages of an open-air school: 'It appears to me,' he says, 'quite as good to give or receive a lesson in the open air as in a stuffy school.'[2]

Pat Frayne's schoolhouse in the townland of Skelgy, County Tyrone, was an equally rude structure. According to Carleton, who was one of his pupils: 'A schoolhouse was built for him – a sod house scooped out of the bank on the roadside – and in the course of a month it was filled with upwards of a hundred scholars, most of them males, but a good number of them females.' Unlike most schools of its kind which were closed during the winter owing to the cold and damp, this one remained open: 'Every winter's day each (scholar) brought two sods of turf for the fire, which was kept burning in the centre of the school: there was a hole in the roof that discharged the functions of a chimney. Around this fire, especially during cold and severe weather, the boys were entitled to sit in a circle by turns... The seats about the fire were round stones.'[3]

However mean the school building, and however great the bodily discomfort of both teacher and scholars, the atmosphere of the Hedge Schools seemed to have been naturally lively and good-humoured. We can gather as much from Carleton's account of his rather depressing experience when he first took charge of a Hedge School.

'I got a promise,' he relates, 'of about a dozen or two wretched boys and girls, and the gift of an uninhabited hut – one of the worst that ever covered a human head. In due time the establishment was opened, and I, William Carleton, became the master of a hedge school. Yes, a hedge school – so it must be called, for so it was. But when I bethought me of the hedge schools in which I had myself been educated, of the multitude assembled, of the din arising from the voices of the comic crew around, I felt like a hermit in a wilderness.'[4]

The schoolmaster had to take what he could get; any shelter was better than none, and what he obtained was usually given to him freely. The people wanted education for their children and very often paid more for it than they could afford. Writing in 1808 of his Irish-speaking tenants in County Sligo, Lord Palmerston said: 'The thirst for education is so great that there are now three or four schools upon the estate. The people join in engaging some itinerant master; they run him up a miserable mud hut on the road side, and the boys pay him half-a-crown, or some five shillings a quarter. They are taught reading, writing and arithmetic, and what, from the appearance of the establishment, no one would imagine, Latin and even Greek.'[5] The same strong desire for education was observed by independent witnesses in other parts of the country; in fact, one writer said that it did more to encourage the efforts of the schoolmaster than anything else. In his 'Statistical Survey of Kildare,' published in 1807, Rawson stated: 'All over the country are numbers of schools, where the lower orders have their children instructed in writing, arithmetic and reading; scarcely a peasant who can muster a crown after tithe and priest's dues, but is emulous to expend it on his little boy's education. No Sunday schools; no encouragement of the neighbouring gentry; no furthering of the benevolent plans of Lancaster.' Yet in spite of lack of all endowment and of patronage, education was widespread: 'The people of

Ireland,' wrote Wakefield a few years later, 'are, I may almost say, universally educated:...I do not know any part of Ireland so wild, that its inhabitants are not anxious, nay, eagerly anxious for the education of their children.'[6]

The willingness of the people to make sacrifices for the education of their children, and their co-operation with the schoolmaster were undoubtedly two of the factors that helped the Hedge School to become a vital force in Irish education.

The Hedge School, such as it was, certainly rendered possible, during the first half of the 18th Century, the conduct of a kind of guerilla warfare in education. In the Report on the 'State of Popery in Ireland in 1731' we find the Bishop of Derry writing to the Lords Committees appointed to enquire into 'ye present state of Popery': 'There are not any Popish schools; sometimes a straggling schoolmaster sets up in some of ye mountainous parts of some parishes, but upon being threatened, as they constantly are, with a warrant, or a presentment by ye Churchwardens, they generally think proper to withdraw.'[7] A note marked 'N.B.' in the returns of the Bishop of Clonfert even better describes the state of affairs: 'By a return made to me at my last visitation there appear'd to be a much greater number of Popish schools than are here return'd. But one of them being taken & convict'd, the rest disappear'd. Many of them have not yet ventur'd to return: And of those who did, some have again absconded upon the first notice of the order of the Lords Committees.'[8]

Thus it happened that education was often found to flourish in remote and mountainous districts. The reputation of the Munster schools and particularly of the schools of Kerry is ample testimony of this.

The classical tradition of the schools of Kerry was evidently of long standing when Dr. Smith wrote in 1756: 'It is well known,' he states, 'that classical learning extends itself, even to a fault, among the lower and poorer kind in this country; many of whom, to the taking them off more useful works, have greater knowledge in this way, than some of the better sort, in other places.' Further he discloses some interesting facts: 'I have in my survey met with some good latin scholars who did not understand the english tongue; particularly one Peter Kelly, who lived in a very uncultivated part of the country... Greek is also taught in some of the mountainous parts, generally by persons who pick it up, as mendicant scholars, at some english school. Neither is the genius of the commonalty confined to this kind of learning alone, for I saw a poor man near Blackstones, who had a tolerable notion of calculating the epacts, golden number, dominical letter, the moon's phases, and even eclipses, altho' he had never been taught to read english.'[9]

The south of Ireland, generally, appears to have had a great number of schools in which Latin was taught. 'The Papists,' wrote Sir James Caldwell in 1764, 'are not only connected by the General Tie of the Religion that acknowledges the Pope for its common Father and Head, with the Courts of France and Spain, but there is not a Family in the Island that has not a relation in the Church, in the Army, or in Trade in those Countries, and in order to qualify the Children for foreign Service, they are all taught Latin in Schools kept in poor Huts, in many Places in the Southern Part of the Kingdom.'[10]

The evidence of classical teaching seems to be more abundant for Kerry than elsewhere; a circumstance that was probably due to its attraction for tourists. We have an anonymous writer in 1776 relating that the poor, ragged boy who held his horse was 'well acquainted with the best Latin poets.'[11] And Holmes in 1797 bears further witness to the continuity of classical learning in Kerry: 'Amongst the uncultivated part of the Country, many may be met with who are all good Latin scholars, yet do not speak a word of English. Greek is also taught in the mountainous parts by some itinerant teachers.'[12]

Weld, in his work on Killarney, is rather inclined to be sceptical. 'Nothwithstanding my earnest endeavours during the time I continued in Kerry,' he states, 'I was unable to procure an interview with one of these learned peasants.' Yet Sir John Carr, an Englishman, found a few years later this 'classical spirit,' as he calls it, very general among 'the lower sort of people' in Kerry.[13] And another Englishman, Dr. Milner, had no difficulty in finding classical scholars, and he actually 'conversed for a considerable time in Latin' with two of them, 'both being indigent schoolmasters.' In a letter written in Latin by one of them to Dr. Milner, he begs permission to address him in Latin – the language of Cicero. He states that, though born of poor parents, he was instructed in Latin and Greek; and that he has known men in the humblest occupations, broom-sellers, coachmen, day-labourers, able to speak Latin well. He says that in order to support his family he keeps a school of forty boys, sons of the peasantry, but youths, very many of them, of great ability and promise. He ends up with a quotation from Juvenal, and, wishing good health and long life to Dr. Milner, signs himself: 'Jacobus Egan.'[14]

The reputation of the schools of Munster was not merely local: From nearly all over Ireland 'poor scholars,' and others who had learned all that they could in their own neighbourhood, and who were not yet satisfied that their education was complete, journeyed thither. There were excellent schools in other parts of the country, but nowhere, it seems, was there within an equal area a greater number of efficient schoolmasters. 'The Munster masters,' wrote Carleton in 1830, 'have long been, and still are, particularly celebrated for making excellent classical and mathematical scholars.'[15]

We do not come upon many references to classical education in the Hedge Schools of the north of Ireland. But it was there for all that. The school of Frank Glass which Dr. Henry Cooke, the Presbyterian divine, attended seems to have been well known. Here is a description of the schoolmaster from the pen of Henry Cooke's biographer: 'He was a pure Milesian, short of stature, fiery in temper, with features exhibiting a strange combination of cunning, thought and humour. He swore at his pupils roundly, and taught them to swear. But he was a good scholar and a successful teacher. Like many of his countrymen, his love for classical literature amounted almost to a passion and he had the rare talent of inspiring favourite pupils with his own enthusiasm. Among Latin authors he delighted in Horace, and down to a recent period Cooke often recited, with intense enjoyment, some of his teacher's quaint renderings of the Odes.'[16]

The Rev. Dr. McIvor sometime Fellow of Trinity College, Dublin, rector of Newtownstewart, vouches for the classical reputation of the country of Tyrone; he says: 'Tyrone has been called, I understand, the Northern Kerry; Kerry may well have been the Southern Tyrone.'[17]

The Rev. Alexander Ross could put in an equally good claim on behalf of the country of Derry. Writing from Dungiven in 1814, he tells us: 'Even in the wildest districts, it is not unusual to meet with good classical scholars; and there are several young mountaineers of the writer's acquaintance, whose knowledge and taste in the Latin poets might put to the blush many who have all the advantages of established schools and regular instruction."[18]

The number of Hedge Schools increased very rapidly during the latter half of the 18th century. This was due, in part only, to the immense growth of the population and to the relaxation of the laws against education; for these were, so to speak, the physical conditions favourable to the spread of education. The real credit must be given to the people themselves, who were determined to have their children instructed. 'The strong passion for education,' stated Mr. John Leslie Foster in a letter to the Secretary of the Board of Education in 1811, 'which... mark(s) the lower classes of our people... assures us, that if we do not assist them, instructed nevertheless they will be.'[19] In 1824 official returns were made of the schools in every Parish in Ireland, and of the children attending each school. Two responsible bodies, the Catholic and Protestant clergy, supplied independently the required figures with what proved to be a remarkable degree of accuracy, for the two returns were practically identical. The number of schools throughout the country were stated to be 11,823 with 561,000 in daily attendance.[20] These returns were made during the three months ending December, 1824. About 2,500 of these were on charitable and private foundations, or connected with one or more of the Protestant Education Societies; all others were independent Pay Schools, that is, schools conducted by private individuals for their own profit and at their own risk. The total number of schools under Catholic teachers was over 8,000 and of these not less than about 7,600 were independent Pay Schools under lay teachers, the remainder being usually schools attached to religious bodies or 'supported by the Collections and Subscriptions of the Roman Catholic Inhabitants of certain Parishes, and under the superintendence of Roman Catholic priests.' A number of these independent Pay Schools were town schools and city 'academies,' but the vast majority of the Pay Schools were truly Hedge Schools, and it was to these that the education of the great bulk of the population was entrusted.

In 1850, Sir Thomas Wyse, stated in a letter to Dr. Doyle, bishop of Kildare and Leighlin,: '... the lower class (in Ireland) proportionally to their position, are better educated than the middle and upper. It is the contrary on the Continent.'[21] From point of view of numbers, the schools in Ireland compared favourably with those in the rest of Europe. The standard of the work done in the Hedge Schools was higher than that done in any other school of equal social status. The curriculum, for one thing, was more extensive; while the attainments of the hedge schoolmaster were usually of a more liberal nature. The very least that was taught in the Hedge Schools included reading, writing and arithmetic. Other subjects found their way into the curriculum according to local needs, and in so far as the qualifications of the teacher would allow: history, geography, book-keeping, surveying and navigation. Latin and Mathematics were commonly taught; sometimes Greek; and in Irish-speaking districts instruction in all these subjects was given in the vernacular. At the beginning of the 19th Century, however, English as a medium of instruction was rapidly replacing Irish; 'amidst some of the wildest mountains of Kerry.' declared Weld in 1806. 'I have met with English schools; and even seen multitudes of children seated round the humble residence of their instructor with their books, pens and ink, where rocks have supplied the place of desks and benches.'[22] It, therefore, happened that in many parts of the country the 'bare-legged peasant,' as Townsend called him, spoke two languages fluently.[23] English was a comparatively recent acquirement at this time; Richard Lovell Edgeworth wrote in 1811: '... they (the Irish peasantry) have within these few years made a greater progress in learning English, than the Welsh have made since the time of Edward the First, in acquiring that language.'[24]

NOTES

1. Printed in Corcoran: State Policy. p. 76.
2. Promenade... dans l'Irlande. p. 107.
3. Autobiography. pp. 19–20.
4. Ibid. pp. 186–7.
5. Quoted by Alice Stopford Green in Irish National Tradition, p. 10.

6. Account of Ireland. Vol. II. p. 307.

7. Printed in Archivium Hibernicum. Vol. I. p. 17.

8. Archivium Hibernicum. Vol. III. p. 133.

9. History of Kerry. pp. 67 and 418.

10. A Brief Examination. 2nd. Ed. p. 27.

11. A Description of Killarney. p. 8.

12. Sketches of the Southern Counties of Ireland. p. 151.

13. The Stranger in Ireland. p. 380.

14. An Inquiry. 2nd. Ed. p. 332.

15. Traits and Stories. 4th Ed. p. 151.

16. Porter: Life... of Henry Cooke. pp. 5–6.

17. Memorial... to Commissioners of National Education, July 25–1867.

18. Mason: Parochial Survey. Vol. I. p. 314.

19. P.P. 1813–4. V. p. 342.

20. P.P. 1826–7. XII. p. 4.

21. Memoirs. p. 16.

22. Killarney. pp. 217–18.

23. Survey of Cork. p. 266.

24. P.P. 1813–14. pp. 339–40.

CHAPTER VI

The Hedge School at Work

One day James Nash, the old hedge schoolmaster said to his friend Thomas Francis Meagher: 'My school is below there, and I flog the boys every morning all round, to teach them to be Spartans.'[1] The extent of the punishment which the gentle old Nash would administer is not actually known, but like McElligott, the Limerick schoolmaster, he would evidently take no excuse for neglect of study. Carleton gives the impression that discipline in the Hedge Schools was not, as a rule, severe; rather the opposite, even when good work was expected of the pupils. In his criticism of the regulations in force in the schools under the National Board of Education, he says: 'I think it a mistake to suppose that silence, among a number of children in school, is conducive to the improvement either of health or intellect. That the chest and lungs are benefited by giving full play to the voice, I think, will not be disputed; and that a child is capable of more intense study and abstraction in the din of a schoolroom, than in partial silence (if I may be permitted the word), is a fact which I think any rational observation would establish. There is something cheering and cheerful in the noise of friendly voices about us – it is a restraint taken off the mind, and it will run the lighter for it–it produces more excitement, and puts the intellect in a better frame of mind for study. The obligation to silence, though it may give the master more ease, imposes a new moral duty upon the child, the sense of which must necessarily weaken his application.' Carleton loved the bustle and busy hum of the schoolroom; he would have the schoolmaster take into serious account the child's natural propensities rather than look to his own personal comfort. He is fully alive to the value of the social factor in education; the boy

45

should work with others: 'Do not send him,' he advises, 'in quest of knowledge alone, but let him have cheerful companionship on his way.' For a very sound reason he does not wish to banish from the schoolroom the schoolboy's joke, his occasional outbursts of merriment in class, or even a little horseplay: 'It is an exercise to the mind,' he asserts, 'and he will return to his business with greater vigour and effect.'

He emphasises some very important aspects of education, which perhaps were neither fully realised nor clearly understood in his day. For example, he points out the need of studying the child-mind: 'Children are not men, nor influenced by the same motives – they do not reflect, because their capacity for reflection is imperfect; so is their reason; whereas, on the contrary, their faculties for education (excepting judgment, which strengthens my argument) are in greater vigour in youth than in manhood. The general neglect of this distinction is, I am convinced, a stumbling block in the way of youthful instruction, though it characterises all our modern systems. We should never forget that they are children, nor should we bind them by a system, whose standard is taken from the maturity of human intellect. We may bend our reason to theirs, but we cannot elevate their capacity of our own. We may produce an external appearance, sufficiently satisfactory to ourselves but, in the meantime, it is probable that the child may be growing in hypocrisy, and settling down into the habitual practice of a fictitious character.' He scorns a system of education that would not produce in the child a spirit of 'honest and manly independence.' He would have the child behave at school with as much freedom as he would in his natural surroundings, and learn as a child would learn in a sympathetic atmosphere. He has little regard for the mechanical methods of teaching which were the distinctive features of the 'mutual system': 'Bell or Lancaster would not relish the pap or caudle-cup three times a day: neither would an infant on the breast feel comfortable after a gorge of ox beef. Let them, therefore, put a little of the mother's milk of human kindness and consideration into their strait-laced systems.' It is not to be thought, however, that the dignity of the teacher should suffer: 'a master should be a monarch in his school, but by no means a tyrant.'[2]

We know very little of the system of teaching in the Hedge Schools but that there was a system is fairly evident from the general agreement between the few vague descriptions of class teaching that are given. A pupil of the old Callan 'Hedge School,' who afterwards became one of the first members of the Irish Christian Brothers, relates his experience of school organisation: 'Our mentor seemed quite oblivious of the economy in time and labour secured by grouping boys of the same standard of knowledge. We were taught individually, and our day was spent almost entirely in 'rehearsing' and 'writing.' Writing meant copying headlines set by our teacher. He did little more than exhort us to 'rehearse' and hear us repeat what we had learnt by 'heart.'[3] Subjects such as writing, arithmetic, mensuration and book-keeping were generally well taught in the Hedge Schools; but unfortunately we find few references to the actual teaching of them and none with any details of value. Townsend, author of the 'Survey of the County of Cork,' published in 1810, writes: 'In these country schools, the masters are often sufficiently competent to their business. Writing and arithmetic are what they usually teach best. In many of them, however, the mode of instruction is altogether ludicrous. All the boys gabble the lesson together as loud and as fast as they can speak, which is called rehearsing. The preceptor when he perceives any one approaching, to show his diligence, enforces this confusion of tongues, and seems to rate the progress of improvement by the scale of vocifera- tion.' In Carleton's sketch, 'The Hedge School,' the teacher instructs his pupils to rehearse in order to impress the passer-by: 'Silence, back from the door, boys, rehearse; every one of you rehearse, I say... till the gentleman goes past.' Writing of the schools of Kilmanaheen, County Clare, the Archdeacon of Kilfenora says that they were 'on an old established plan, reading aloud or humming together.'[4] Though the evidence here indicates the prevalence of rehearsing in the schools, Townsend, a most uncompromising critic of the Hedge Schools definitely implies that it was not universal; indeed it might have been general only in the poorer class of Hedge Schools. It had, however, its uses. Where books and writing materials were too expensive for the children to purchase, learning by heart was an economy as well as an obvious aid to retaining information. Again, there was much subject matter which could not be obtained except from costly text-books: but this the schoolmaster usually acquired for himself in the first instance, and then taught to his class sometimes with the aid of manuscript copies, more often without. Further, rehearsing kept the school occupied as a whole, and helped to maintain a show of discipline and industry in the classroom.

A teacher of one of the London Hibernian Society's schools gives an interesting description of *his* day's work: 'Our school begins precisely at ten o'clock in the morning for we cannot begin earlier, as many of the children come from a distance. Every child must be in his seat by that time. I then open the school by reading a psalm or hymn. After that, they all repeat a task to me, of grammar or spelling, and then a lesson in classes, for I have them all classed together according to their several abilities. About twenty of the children write on paper, twenty on slate, and twenty on sand.

'After writing they all have a lesson, and a task of scripture verses which they commit to memory. I have now many good monitors, who assist me very much. I wish you could send me some premiums for them. The labour of the day is concluded by reading a psalm, and making a few remarks of a religious nature, suitable to the subject, and adapted to their capacities, to which they listen with great attention.'[5]

The main features of the plan of work seem to be individual examination of prescribed lessons, grouping of scholars according to their attainments, the practice of committing matter to memory, and the employment of monitors to lighten the work of the teacher. It is maintained that in the Hedge Schools there was no such thing as grouping children in classes; all pupils were taught individually. But here was a rival of the Hedge Schools with the grouping system in full swing, taught by a man to whom the hedge schoolmaster was not in the least inferior. As for the monitorial system, Carleton declares that it was in common use in the Hedge Schools; he has a good deal to say in favour of the system as it was employed in the Hedge Schools: 'I know not whether the Commissioners of Education found the monitorial system of instruction in such of the old hedge schools as maintained an obstinate resistance to the innovations of modern plans. That Bell and Lancaster deserve much credit for applying and extending the principle (I speak without reference to its merits) I do not hesitate to grant; but it is unquestionably true, that the principle was reduced to practice in Irish hedge schools long before either of these worthy gentlemen were in existence. I do not, indeed, at present remember whether or not they claim it as a discovery, or simply as an adaptation of a practice which experience, in accidental cases, had found useful, and which they considered capable of more extensive benefit. I remember many instances, however, in which it was applied – and applied, in my opinion, though not as a permanent system, yet more judiciously than it is at present.'[6] It is contended that what Carleton refers to here was the practice of appointing a boy, who had finished his ordinary schooling and who wished to continue his studies, as usher or assistant, such as Patrick Lynch was at the Rev. Mr.

49

Hare's school, or Richard McElligott at the Limerick school where he first began to learn classics. But anyone who has had experience of a country National school under one teacher, and with an average attendance of fifty, say, will remember that it was usual for the teacher to put two or three of the older boys in charge of junior classes, while he himself was engaged with a particular class. At the end of the lesson the teacher briefly examined each class, sending the senior boys in turn back to their ordinary work at which they remained until he needed them again. These boys, who were selected for their special abilities in reading, writing, arithmetic or other subjects, often spent as much as half their day in teaching. And it was purely an honorary post though much sought after. I am inclined to think that this practice was somewhat of the nature of the monitorial system in the old Hedge Schools; but where the 'poor scholar' took a hand, it was rather in the capacity of an usher or assistant master, though an unpaid one.

References to teaching are seldom come upon. Carleton boasts that he learned his letters in a single day.: 'It was while we lived in Towney that I was first sent to school. I remember the occasion well. I could not have been more than six or seven years of age, and until that day I had never seen a letter of the alphabet. The reader may judge of the surprise of my family when they found on my return that I had not only learned the alphabet, both large letters and small, but had actually got as far as *b-a-g* – bag.[7] Daniel O'Connell, at the age of four, had done better than that; he learned the whole alphabet from David Mahony, a wandering schoolmaster, in the space of an hour and a half, 'perfectly and permanently.'[8]

A contemporary, one of the Commissioners of the Board of Education of 1825, complains of the 'mechanical and laborious methods by which the memory is exercised,' adding that the 'understanding and moral powers' seem to have no claim upon the teacher's attention. His attack is directed mainly to the Hedge Schools: 'In the ordinary pay schools, and above all in that poorest class, formerly called Hedge Schools, we do not look for an intelligent system of instruction; the teacher himself is too ignorant, or, if naturally endowed, has not the ability to exercise the minds of his pupils.'[9] These charges could not be generally true. Taking, for instance, Peter Galleghan as an example of the teacher of the poorest class of school, we find that he has written down in his own hand notes on the most up-to-date methods of teaching the ordinary school subjects – reading, grammar, arithmetic, etc., and much information on various topics which showed that he kept well abreast of the times. The country schoolmaster who taught the Griffins at Fairy Lawn 'was a man of great integrity, of very industrious habits, an excellent English scholar, a good Grammarian, and wrote a beautiful hand.' Pat Frayne and O'Beirne, two of Carleton's teachers, were both excellent at their work; that, at any rate, is the reputation which Carleton gives them. Many of the Hedge Schools were attended by the children of Protestant parents sometimes in preference to sending them to schools run by teachers of their own denomination. The popularity of the schoolmaster to whom pupils came from other parts of the country, was based upon his ability to teach as well as upon his wit and knowledge. 'To exercise the minds' of its pupils would seem to have been one of the traditional aims of the Hedge Schools; that is, if one may judge by the schoolmaster's fondness of displaying his own learning, and of proving his ingenuity in argument. You remember the schoolmaster in 'The Deserted Village.':

> 'In arguing, too, the parson own'd his skill,
> For e'en though vanquish'd, he could argue still.'

A ready tongue, a quick wit were weapons which often proved invaluable to the hedge schoolmaster; and woe to the reputation of the teacher whom they failed at a critical moment! We are told that when a barefooted peasant boy was rebuked for reading the classics as so much waste of time, he replied: 'Est quodam prodire tenus, si non datur ultra' – an answer that should have confounded and silenced his critic.

The kind of text-book used in the Hedge Schools is a fair indication of the methods of teaching employed. Wall's 'Hibernian Preceptor' contains in the list of subscribers the names of over a hundred teachers, many of whom were hedge schoolmasters. The first eleven lessons in this work deal with 'The Elements of Spelling' and give examples of 'the most common and general sounds of the letters, and which children should be habituated to before they enter into the various changes of sound which the same letters should have.'

The Reading Lessons begin on page 47; and here we find, in the first two sentences of Lesson 1, a statement to the effect that spelling came before reading: 'It is a fine thing to know how to read; but we must know how to spell first. We cannot read till we can spell.' Then after long lists of words of two syllables, which the scholar is expected to have mastered, comes the assurance: 'Now that I have learned to spell better; I hope I shall be able, and may read better now.' The Archdeacon of Ferns was shocked to find that this order was not followed in the Hedge Schools in the parishes of Adamstown and Newbawn, County Wexford: 'Here,' he wrote, 'an attempt is made to teach them to read before they can spell, and to write before they can read.'[10] It is probable that the teachers in these schools realised the advantages of teaching reading, spelling and writing concurrently, and were deliberately acting according to what they believed to be a better plan.

In the teaching of arithmetic the method of work seems to have been very carefully devised. In Deighan's Arithmetic, each rule is clearly given, and followed by two sets of examples, the first of which consists of carefully graduated problems while the second contains more difficult questions. 'In forming the first collection of examples,' we find it stated, 'the Author has scrupulously avoided the inadvertence of former writers, by rendering them unembarrassing and easy, and rising in such a gradual succession, without the anticipation of any subsequent rule, as scarcely to require the tutor's assistance, except now and then to explain the nature of the process and examine the truth of the operation.' The writer is also aware of the value of the correlation of arithmetic with other subjects, for he adds: 'by these examples a great accession of knowledge will be acquired in Chronology, History, Mechanics, Astronomy, and the useful Sciences.' The treatment of the rules is very lucid, particularly of those dealing with fractions. His handling of the decimalisation of money compares very favourably with modern methods.

Deighan's Geography was the fruit of his own personal investigation and observation; a fact to which he calls attention in the preface. Lynch in his own text book of Geography emphasises the value of the exercise of reasoning and judgment, and the importance of research in the study of geography. We have proof, too, that mathematics as taught in the Hedge Schools was of an eminently practical nature: when Dr. Hincks was giving evidence before the Education Committee in 1835, he was asked the question: 'Are you aware that, in making an ordnance survey in Ireland, great facility existed in finding competent persons to assist the surveyors at ordinary labourers' wages?' and he answered: 'I have not heard the circumstance before; but from what I saw of the country people in the south of Ireland, and the desire for knowledge amongst them, I am not at all surprised at the circumstance; there were a great many of the hedge schools, where there was given a great deal of scientific instruction.'[11]

To show that the Irish schoolmaster had a keen appreciation of advance in methods of teaching, we may cite the 'recommendatory letter' given above the names of McElligott, O'Brien, Geoghagan, and other Limerick teachers, published in the 'Limerick Gazette' of Feb. 2. 1813, shortly after the appearance of the third edition of Deighan's arithmetic:

'We, the undernamed, being always anxious for the prosperity of our Pupils, do request their Parents to provide them with Mr. Deighan's *Third Edition of his Universal Arithmetic*, as being the only Book extant whereby Youth can acquire a knowledge and facility of the most modern and concise methods of Counting-house calculations. Should we be induced by prejudice or ancient customs to continue *Gough* or *Voster* in our Schools, to us it may be said, that we wish to deprive those committed to our care of the invaluable advantages contained in this Work. *Gough* and *Voster* deserved well in their day, but their methods are now become too tedious and elaborate, and are totally exploded in every Counting-house of eminence. We should deem it reprehensible and incompatible with the honest discharge of our duties, did we not thus publicly declare our sentiments; and we further add, that no other Treatise on Arithmetic, but Mr. Deighan's, shall meet our sanction or support in our Schools, until such time as we shall see (*if* possible) another which shall add more to the improvement of our Pupils.'

NOTES

1. Griffith: Meagher. p. 288.
2. Traits and Stories. Vol. II. pp. 219–222.
3. Edmund Ignatius Rice. p. 49.
4. Mason: Parochial Survey. Vol. I. 495.
5. Fifth Report. p. 20.
6. Traits and Stories. Vol. II. pp. 218–19.
7. Autobiography. pp. 11–12.
8. O'Connell: Life... of Daniel O'Connell. Vol. I. p. 6.
9. Glassford: Popular Education in Ireland. pp. 12, 20.
10. Mason: Parochial Survey. Vol. I. p. 5.
11. P.P. 1836. XIII. p. 20.

CHAPTER VII

The Standard of Knowledge Attained

In a document, dated April 9 1789, containing the private report of Dr. Curtis, Rector of the Irish College at Salamanca, we find entries such as the following:

'Dn. Patricio Mangan, a student. A native of the Arch-diocese, of Dublin, of Catholic and Noble parents, 22 years of age, he has enjoyed a burse for four years. He made much progress in his native land in Latin, Greek, French and other branches of Humanities. In this College, he has studied Hebrew, Mathematics and Philosophy, and is at present in First Year's Theology; in all this, he has progressed commensurately with his great talents, application, and excellent conduct. He is a youth of great promise.'[1]

Nearly all the students mentioned in this report 'had learned the Humanities very well at home,' or 'had learned sufficient Humanities at home to enter this college.' Altogether there were at Salamanca in 1789 twenty-six such students from nearly as many counties in Ireland; and, since the Irish College had been incorporated with the University of Salamanca in 1608, the qualifications for entrance must in many cases have been of corresponding university standard. Further, from the number of Irishmen who received important official appointments on the Continent and secured University professorships, their early training must have been sufficiently sound to enable them to profit by University teaching. Dr. Milner was convinced that 'the Irish students in the foreign universities, down to the very period of the late revolution, carried off more than a due proportion of prizes and professorships, by the sheer merit of superior talents and learning, and a much greater proportion than fell to the lot of all other foreigners put together.'[2]

Carleton tells us that by the age of thirteen or fourteen he had '*only* got as far as Ovid's 'Metamorphoses,' Justin and the first chapter of John in the Greek Testament.' This was after a period of three years under Charles McGoldrick in a school at Tulnavert. Considering that at this time it was the custom to put scholars through the grammar and syntax of each language before giving them a text-book, this might be regarded as an achievement; though Carleton does not seem to look upon it as such himself.

Education was largely a question of opportunity. Where instruction was to be had and where it could be availed of, the results seem to have been generally satisfactory. Thomas Reid, an Englishman travelling in Ireland in 1822, a writer of independent judgment, observes that 'it is not unusual for members of the same family to devote themselves to all the grovelling toil of husbandry, without being able to show even a little reading and writing, while another more fortunate in education displays an accurate knowledge of the Greek and Latin classics.'[3]

Crofton Croker found a knowledge of classics to be quite general in the south of Ireland. 'Among the peasantry,' he writes, 'classical learning is not uncommon and a tattered Ovid or Virgil may be found even in the hands of common labourers.'[4] But he gives no idea of the standard attained.

This, indeed, appears to have been an uncertain quantity, varying from school to school. In giving evidence before the Select Committee on Education in Ireland in 1835, the Rev. Dr. Bryce a Protestant clergyman, Principal of the Belfast Academy, stated in reference to classical teaching in Ireland that he considered the standard of Latin prose composition inferior to that in Scotland, and probably to that in England; but he added: 'I ought to notice, however, that I have found young men intended for the Roman-catholic priesthood, much superior to any others in Ireland in respect of Latin prose composition.'[5] Now, since many of those entering the Church were bound to be products of the Hedge Schools, it follows that classics were at the very least as well taught in the Hedge Schools as in any other school in Ireland.

While the teaching of Latin continued to claim attention, the study and use of Irish would seem to have been declining. Anderson points out that of the three great Celtic speaking races of the British Isles only the Irish were losing grip of their native language; Gaelic was being studied more intensely in the highlands of Scotland, and the use of the vernacular was becoming more wide-spread in Wales.[6] Ever since the timer of Henry VIII the use of Irish was expressly discouraged, though Queen Elizabeth I certainly approved of translations into Irish of the Book of Common Prayer and the New Testament, but not with a view to enable the people to read their own language. In later years Bedell's translation of the Bible appeared, but again with a religious, not an educational, purpose.

At the beginning of the 19th Century a more determined effort on the part of the English Government in Ireland was made to employ the language as a medium of instruction, for it was believed that there were about one and a half millions of people who *spoke* no other language but Irish. It was pointed out that it would entail much less expense to teach these people to read in their own native tongue and then use that as a basis for the study of English, than to teach them English at once. Further, the language was looked upon as a religious barrier as well as a racial barrier.

In 1824, there were considerably over two million people who *commonly used* the Irish language. This was a remarkable number considering that it had rather become the fashion for some time to eschew the language in favour of English. That it still remained so vigorous was due partly to tradition and partly to the conservative character of the Irish peasantry. There were parts of the country where the people manifested no desire to learn the English language. It was such places that Dewar had in mind when he wrote: 'Everyone had heard of the hedge schools, so common in Ireland, where crowds of poor children on the side of the road are taught to read and write. In every instance where the Irish language is taught, and where there is no offence given to the prejudices of the natives, parents discover the utmost solicitude to have their offspring instructed, and almost universally send them to school.'[7] Another writer, Mr. J. B. Trotter, sometime private secretary to Charles James Fox, the famous English statesman, noted particularly the lack of books in Irish-speaking districts: 'Books in Irish are not to be had...' he stated. 'The best authors – the noble ancient poets drest in their own interesting and expressive native language, would be greedily read by the Irish who had received any education. For their sensibility, quickness, and comprehension of intellect are truly admirable!'[8]

Printed text-books in the Irish language were rare and expensive. A grammar of the Irish language, an English-Irish dictionary and grammar, a Catechism 'in the Irish language and character, with corresponding pages in English,' were all printed on the Continent during the 18th Century. About the same time Dr. Gallagher's sermons were published in Dublin, as were the catechisms one in English and one in Irish of Dr. O'Reilly, bishop of Armagh: while an Irish-English dictionary was published in Paris by Dr. John O'Bryan, bishop of Cloyne. Some of these went through several editions, and some of them certainly found their way into the hands of hedge schoolmasters in Irish-speaking districts of the South and West.

That these schoolmasters were fond of imparting to their pupils the best that was in them we have certain evidence. Some of them boasted of having produced the most renowned Irish scholars in the country. Eugene Cavanagh, the Limerick schoolmaster and poet, writing about 1825, expressed a high opinion of the attainments of one of his pupils: 'Patrick Carroll, a pupil of mine now living in Ballinstona, between Kilmallock and Bruff, is certainly the ablest and most universal Irish linguist that I know now in existence.'[9] And while teachers were proud of distinguished pupils, pupils were no less proud of having been taught by teachers of repute. 'It is a curious fact,' wrote Dr. Standish O'Grady in 1853, 'that almost every Irish scholar who has appeared at either side of the Comeragh mountains for more than the last eighty years, has been a pupil of Donnchadh himself or one of those instructed by him.'[10]

In many parts of the country the people spoke two languages well. For example, in West Cork 'the lower class of people,' according to Newenham,[11] 'for the most part, spoke English as fluently as the Irish language.' English they used in business affairs, while Irish was the language of the home and the fields.

The hedge schoolmaster was often proud of his English. In the home parents were particularly careless of imparting a knowledge of Irish to their children; in fact, they sometimes looked upon the ignorance of the younger generation in this respect as an advantage when they wished to discuss private affairs in their hearing. Yet the schoolmaster must have deplored what was happening, for every now and then we find him either defiantly singing the praises of the language or regretting its decay. He has been instrumental, however, in the preservation of thousands of legends, songs and poems, and in helping to perpetuate the use of his native tongue.

Besides Latin and Irish, there was another subject in which the Hedge Schools showed a good deal of proficiency. This was Mathematics, which, in one way or other, was taught in every school.

Richard Lovell Edgeworth is very emphatic in his opinion of the respective arithmetical attainments of the children of poor parents and the sons of the well-to-do.

59

He writes: 'I rely upon the event of any trials that may be made upon boys of the higher and lower classes in Ireland, in which I am certain it will be found that not only the common, but the higher parts of Arithmetic are better understood and more expertly practised by boys without shoes and stockings, than by young gentlemen riding home on horseback or in coaches, to enjoy their Christmas idleness.'[12]

Carleton informs us that he himself 'got a tolerably good notion of Gough's Arithmetic' though he is careful to point out that he had no taste for Mathematics. Speaking of Pat Frayne, the hedge schoolmaster, he says: 'My brother John made a first-rate arithmatician; but Pat could never succeed in that direction with me. I had no genius for science, nor was I ever able to work out a proposition of Euclid during my life.'

Glassford found that Arithmetic was one of the most popular of school subjects. 'Arithmetic,' he writes in one place, 'is a favourite branch of instruction with the Irish people generally.' In another place he calls it 'the Irishman's hobby.'[13] Not alone was there considerable attention given to it at school, but it was studied with interest afterwards. Carleton tells us of 'a man who kept a public-house,' who was so interested in mathematics that he 'corresponded for years, in the mathematical department, with one of these small publications which went among the lower classes at that time – sometimes called 'The Lady's Almanack,' and sometimes 'The Lady's Magazine.' These were annuals which had a section devoted to mathematical problems, the questions being inserted one year, and the solutions being given the following issue. Such distinguished men as Professor McCullough of Trinity College, Dublin, and the late Lord Kelvin's father were noted contributors to them in their day.

Bicheno, author of a book entitled, 'Ireland and its Economy,' published in 1830, suggests a reason for the study of Arithmetic in Hedge Schools. 'In the common

Catholic schools,' he states, 'arithmetic and geometry were carried to some length'; to which he adds in a footnote: 'The inducement to study these seems to be the practical application of them in measuring land, which is carried to such minuteness, as seems rediculous to those who have been used to see farms of 500 and 600 acres.'

The evidence of the Rev. Dr. Hincks with regard to progress of mathematics and science in the Hedge Schools is extremely important. Dr. Hincks was well qualified to speak on the subject; he had had considerable experience in teaching in the south of Ireland. From 1790 to 1815 he taught in the city of Cork; and from 1815 to 1821 in Fermoy, at which date he was appointed principal of the Belfast Academical Institution, a position he still held in 1835. 'I have known instances,' he stated, 'of very considerable advance in science, especially in mathematics, in the very lowest schools. I have known persons procuring scientific books, and apparently able to make use of those books, who were in very great poverty, in the south of Ireland especially. I think there is much more of such taste for scientific acquirements in the south than in the north.'[14]

1. Archivium Hibernicum. Vol. IV. p. 53.
2. An Inquiry. p. 16.
3. Travels in Ireland in 1882. p. 243.
4. Researches. p. 326.
5. P.P. 1836. XIII. p. 2.
6. Memorial on behalf of the Native Irish. p. 6.
7. Observations on the Character... of the Irish. p. 139.
8. Walks thro' Ireland. p. 46.
9. Catalogue of Irish MSS. in the British museum. Vol. II. p. 179.
10. Introd. to 'Adventures of Donnchadh Ruadh Mac Con Mara'. p. 4.
11. Author of 'A View... of Ireland'. 1809.
12. Letter to Lord Selkirk, 1808. Printed in 'The Black Book of Edgeworthstown,' p. 104 et seq.
13. Tours in Ireland. pp. 2, 66.
14. P.P. 1836. XIII. p. 20.

CHAPTER VIII

School Books

To the great mass of the people the price of books was prohibitive. A shilling in Irish money represented, in the most prosperous part of the country, a full day's wage for a farm labourer; in poorer districts it would have paid three days' wages. For that reason alone books were rarely bought, and for the same reason the possession of a few books was a thing to be proud of.

An advertisement in the 'Ennis Chronicle' of March 3rd, 1793, gives some idea of the price of books at this period:

'RATIONAL SPELLING BOOK

'Just published by the printer hereof, a New and improved Edition of the Rational Spelling Book, price 1s. 7½d.; Watt's ditto, 1s. 7½d.; Universal ditto, 1s. 1d. ... Dowling's Book-keeping, Voster's Arithmetick, with an extensive assortment of School Books...'

Unfortunately, none of such advertisements gives a more complete list of the books commonly used in the schools. The above were probably popular prices. Other books were more expensive. Bonnycastle's Arithmetic cost 2s., Patrick Lynch's Irish Grammar was advertised at 3s. 3d., and Deighan's Geography of Ireland cost 6s.; text-books which few scholars could afford to buy.

There were a number of works on arithmetic in general use. Voster's Arithmetic was the oldest. This was superseded by Gough's and the latter, in the early part of the 19th century, by Thompson's. On seeing a copy of Gough's Arithmetic in the hands of a well known teacher, Carleton affected to be shocked: 'Gough's,' he exclaimed... 'Surely it is not possible that you are teaching the system of a man who for years has proved himself to be ignorant of the doctrine of proportion! I thought I should have found Thompson here, not Gough – but indeed, Mr. Newland, I did expect to have met you with Homer or Virgil in your hand, and not with such a schoolboy's book as Gough's Arithmetic.' There was also an Arithmetic by Darling in use in the Blue Coat Hospital, Dublin; and judging by the number of 'Recommendatory Letters' which its author received from teachers throughout the country Deighan's Arithmetic must have enjoyed great popularity. As regards the other branches of mathematics, it seems that Bonnycastle's Geometry and Algebra, Simpson's Euclid, Keith's Trigonometry, and others of equal merit were in the hands of a great many schoolmasters. Bonnycastle was among the books of Thomas Ruadh O'Sullivan, the poet-schoolmaster; and Lynch had obviously a sound knowledge of Keith's mathematical works. Bonnycastle and Keith were teachers of note in their day; the former taught at the Royal Military Academy, Woolwich, the latter described himself as 'Private Teacher of Mathematics.'

There were also text-books of history, geography, the use of the globes, and navigation, the latter being particularly in evidence in schools in or near seaport towns.

Text-books were as we have seen occasionally written by Irish schoolmasters and knowing how difficult it was to put any book on the market, we cannot but admire their industry and courage. Sometimes the manuscript of a work was submitted in turn to those who were likely to subscribe to it. It is pleasing to note, however, that in lists of subscribers the names of teachers are usually in the majority. Lynch was author of many notable works; Deighan wrote text-books of geography, book-keeping, algebra, and arithmetic; George Wall, stated to be 'Teacher of Reading, Elocution, Geography, published at Parsontown (Birr) etc.,' in 1810 the first volume of 'The Hibernian Preceptor,' and the second volume two years later at Dublin. No doubt most of these books found their way into both town and country schools.

The lack of text-books of arithmetic, book-keeping geography, and other subjects, was not a serious handicap to the scholar, for he had at his disposal all that his teacher knew. Usually, the schoolmaster who undertook to teach these subjects had sufficient knowledge for the purpose; and even when he could not afford to buy the latest text-books, he had in manuscript form the most up-to-date information both as regards matter and method obtained by himself from a variety of sources. The large folios written by some of the schoolmasters are evidence of this. There is some reason to believe that these were occasionally sold to other teachers, for in the manuscript of Peter Galleghan, possessed by the Edinburgh University Library, the author gives a broad hint that it is worth at least five pounds.

The attention of contemporary writers is almost entirely directed to the reading books found in the Hedge Schools. Dutton, for example, gives a list of the readers he discovered in use in the schools of County Clare. 'The state of education,' he wrote, 'may be easily appreciated, when it is known that, with the exception of a few universal spelling books, the general cottage classics are:

History of the Seven Champions of Christendom.
– Montelion, Knight of the Oracle.
– Parisimus and Parismenes.
– Irish Rogues and Rapparees.
– Freney, a notorious robber, teaching them the
   most dangerous mode of robbing.
– the most celebrated pirates.
– Jack the Bachelor, a noted smuggler.
– Fair Rosamund and Jane Shore, two prostitutes.
– Donna Rosina, a Spanish Courtesan.
– Ovid's Art of Love.
– History of Witches and Apparitions.

64

    – The Devil and Dr. Faustus.

    – Moll Flanders – highly edifying, no doubt.

    – New System of Boxing, by Mendoza, etc., etc.'

    He also mentions 'Alibaba,' and a book entitled, 'Seven Sleepers.'[1]

Wakefield, writing about four years later, quotes Dutton's list at full length, and adds: 'the books which Mr. Dutton enumerates are common. I met with nearly a similar list in Wicklow; and I found such, or as bad, in very general use.'[2] Another contemporary, giving information concerning the schools of the parish of Kilrush, County Clare in 1816, writes in the same vein: 'The hedge schools are as miserable, and the books in them as worthless as they have been observed to be in other parts of Ireland. Indeed so universally similar are the latter in this country, that a list of those found at the schools here in 1808, served to enumerate those at present used in one of the northern parishes.'[3] It seems rather a pity that the last two writers do not strike an original note, and give the names of the better types of book found in the Hedge Schools, instead of taking their cue from Mr. Hely Dutton.

Carleton is particularly critical of the reading books used by school children: 'The matter placed in their hands,' he states, 'was of a most inflammatory and pernicious nature, as regarded politics; and as far as religion and morality were concerned, nothing could be more gross and superstitious than the books which circulated among them.'[4]

Carleton gives a long list of these books. Most of them were probably the cheap reprints issued at Dublin, Limerick, and Cork, and known as the 'Burton Books,' or 'sixpenny books.' In Dublin no less than four booksellers, we are told, were engaged in the sole business of issuing them, and one bookseller had four printing presses; altogether some 300,000 books were published annually, and circulated throughout the country mainly by hawkers who invariably did a flourishing trade in them. Parents undoubtedly bought some of these books, for they were the cheapest on the market, and handed them on to their children when the latter required something to read from at school. In fact it was these books, or nothing.

The London Hibernian Society regarded the books they found in the Hedge Schools as 'nonsensical... containing Fairy Tales, the History of St. Patrick, the Seven Champions of Christendom, the Scapular, &c.' or at the very best Aesop's Fables.' The Hibernian Bible Society called them 'foolish legends which poisoned the minds of youth.' Other semi-religious bodies endeavoured to suppress these 'licentious books,' as they were pleased to call them. The earliest efforts of the 'Association for Discountenancing Vice and Promoting the Knowledge and Practice of the Christian Religion' were directed to this end; the Association had recourse first to moral suasion, and finding that no use brought the law to their aid in order to induce the hawkers to abandon their trade in these books. The Kildare Place Society based their plans on a much sounder footing; they sought to supplant them by providing other books. They issued a series of reprints, on the sale of which they allowed a wide margin of profit, fourpence in the shilling, to hawkers. It is stated that, as a result, they got hold of the market in cheap books, and finally of the printing presses. This is scarcely correct, for the books against which their campaign was undertaken were in vogue at a much later date; indeed, it was not until after 1824 that they were called 'Chap Books', and Thackeray mentions them in 'The Irish Sketch-Book.' The Cheap Book Society also published books, which were not bibles or tracts, to take the place of the 'sixpenny books.' In its first printed report, the Society announces the success of their efforts: 'the avidity amongst the lower orders of this people for mental improvement keeps full pace with the generous labours of their benefactors and instructors.'[5]

In Mason's 'Parochial Survey of Ireland' there are a good many references to the readers used in the Hedge Schools. The facts in each case are supplied by the local clergyman of the Established Church. It is stated that in Kilmore, County Roscommon, 'the books in general use are, the common spelling books, short histories, or other narratives, and the usual authors on Arithmetic, such as Voster and Gough.' In Errigal-Keroge, County Tyrone, it would appear that no particular book was employed as a reader for the schools: 'The mixture of books that the children use is a great impediment to improvement at these schools. The spelling-books are of various kinds and bad sorts; and the books for those advanced to reading, are generally those sold by pedlars of odd volumes of novels.' In connection with the Hedge Schools of Middleton, County Cork, we find it stated that 'the books generally read in these schools are Catholic.' In the Survey of Rathline, County Longford, the report points out: 'The books they (the children) read are not calculated to impress on their tender minds either a sence of religion or virtue; they are generally story-books, or some vulgar ill-written histories.' The compiler of the Survey of Tracton Abbey, County Cork, makes no comment on the value of the books used in the parish schools. 'In each parish,' he writes, 'there is at least one (school), kept by a Roman Catholic master, and in which the children learn to read in such books as their parents may have, including every variety, from the 'History of Reynard the Fox' to 'Chesterfield's Rules of Politeness.'

At least one writer, other than Carleton, draws attention to the fact that political pamphlets found their way into the schools, and were used as reading books. The Rev. Robert Shaw in the Survey of Tullaroan, published in 1819, states: 'the books used, are the common primer, and the universal spelling-book. Books for reading in, are very few in number, and of that description well known to those who examine the books which pedlars and petty shop-keepers sell to the country people, such as the histories of robbers, &c., and particularly that pernicious little book, 'the Articles of Limerick,' of which several thousand copies are sold every year throughout every part of the nation, which it is impossible for children to read without imbibing a spirit of disloyalty to the government, and hatred to the present royal family and English connection.' A book that would have caused this writer more anxiety still was a little text entitled: 'A Sketch of Irish History by Way of Question and Answer for the Use of Schools.' This must have been well known to schoolmasters, though only one reference to it has been met with. The Commissioners of the Board of Education reported in 1825 that they saw a copy of it in one of the schools established by the Christian Brothers.

The preface to this book explains its object: 'The complete neglect,' writes the author, 'of giving children any information on the subject of the history of Ireland, in most instances: and the general misrepresentation in those cases, where it has been touched upon gave rise to the following Sketch. The expression of truth in the most concise terms and in language suited to the capacities of those for whom the work is designed, was the only object kept in view. How far this has been attained must be decided by the Judgement of the Public.'

The study of history was completely discouraged in the schools. The absence of books of history in the various schools was part of a well defined policy. Richard Lovell Edgeworth explains: 'I have been told, that in some schools the Greek and Roman histories are forbidden; such abridgements of these histories as I have seen are certainly improper; to inculcate democracy and a foolish hankering after undefined liberty, is not necessary in Ireland.'[6] Taking their cue from this leading authority on education, contemporary writers are emphatic in their opinions that the teaching of history, particularly in the Hedge Schools, laid the foundations of discontent, and of disaffection to constituted government. All reading matter was to be suppressed, except what was specifically intended to inculcate 'piety and morality, and industry.'

There is evidence of the existence of readers of the definitely 'school book' type. 'The Priests...' states an agent of the London Hibernian Society, 'endeavoured to persuade their audience to withdraw their children from any teacher who would not teach them in the 'Reading made Easy'; 'Childs' New Play Thing,' &c., &c.' The two mentioned here occur in the list of the 'sixpenny books' published in Dublin. No doubt, there were many such school books which Dutton, Carleton and others have omitted to mention.

The charges which these writers level against the books in the hands of the children attending the Hedge Schools are manifestly unjust. In the first place, very few of the books were really bad in themselves, they were mostly romantic tales; and, secondly, they were never used as class books; each child read his lesson from the book he happened to possess at the time, and that was the end of the matter as far as the teacher was concerned. Indeed, it might well have happened that there were as many different reading books in the school as there were children who read. 'It has occurred to a Member of our Commission,' states a Report of the Commissioners of the Board of Education in 1825, 'to see, in a School in the County of Sligo, a Child holding the New Testament in Its Hands, sitting between Two others, one of whom was supplied with the 'Forthy Thieves,' and the other with 'the Pleasant Art of Money Catching,' while another at a little Distance was perusing the 'Mutiny Act,' and all reading aloud their respective Volumes at the same Moment.'[7] The view that such works were never employed as class books is supported by Fitzgibbon, one of the masters of Chancery in Ireland, who wrote in 1868: 'Both the Commissioners of 1806 and of 1824 animadverted on the pay schools which then existed, observing, that the instruction afforded by them was extremely limited, and the masters, in general, very ill-qualified to give even that instruction, having themselves been taught in schools of a similar description. That, instead of being improved by moral and religious instruction the minds of the pupils were corrupted by books calculated to incite to lawless and profligate adventure, to cherish superstition, or to lead to dissension or disloyalty (*vide* Report 1825, p. 38).

'This stricture on the schools and the books was founded on evidence, that certain books mentioned by some of the witnesses were used in those old schools; among them the lives of two Irish highwaymen, named Freny and O'Hanlon, which appear to be the books alluded to as inciting to lawless and profligate adventure. It should have been noticed that no one of these books so objected to ever was a school-book, in any school. They were twopenny romances, which boys bought with their pocket-money, and read for mere amusement; and many of them, if not all, were of a very harmless character. Being voluntarily read, in addition to the school tasks, they promoted ability to read, which was some set-off against the assumed moral ill affects of them.'[8]

The Report of the Board of Education of 1825 gives a remarkable list of books found by the Commissioners in common use in schools, a very great number of which were books of sound literary and historical value. In addition to those given under the headings of 'Cathechism' and 'Religious Works,' there are beneath the title, 'Works of Entertainment, Histories, Tales, etc.,' such books as – I give a selection – Don Quixote, The Vicar of Wakefield, Hume's History of England, Drake's Voyages, Travels to the North Sea, Life of Buonaparte, Mme. de Sévigné's Letters, etc., etc. We might, therefore, go a little further than Fitzgibbon, and say that the schools had at their disposal a sufficient variety of books not only to enable practically every child to read, but also to give opportunities, to many of them, of acquiring a taste for literature and history.

NOTES

1. Survey of Clare. pp. 236-8.
2. Account of Ireland. Vol. II. p. 401.
3. Mason: Parochial Survey. Vol. II. p. 465.
4. Traits and Stories. Vol. II. pp. 234-6.
5. Printed in Shaw: Survey of Tullaroan. p. 148.
6. Letter to Committee of the Board of Education. P.P. 1813-14. V. p. 109.
7. P.P. 1825. XII. p. 44.
8. Ireland in 1868. pp. 76-7.

CHAPTER IX

The Making of the Schoolmaster

Those who took up teaching as a profession had generally some claim to distinction in learning. We find one schoolmaster referred to as the best classical scholar in Munster, another as possessing an excellent knowledge of Irish, a third as one of the best book-keepers of his day in the North of Ireland, and so on. We know definitely that some were distinguished poets, that several were writers of important works on languages, history, geography, mathematics, and other subjects, while not a few were authorities in their own branches of study.

We find, too, that it was because of their superior knowledge that many young men became schoolmasters; for instance, in a statement on the condition of education in Dungiven, County Derry, we learn that 'private schools in almost every townland... are kept in general by the native Irish, who having pursued their taste for literature... can afterwards find no other employment for their talents or acquirements.'[1] It is certain also that many qualified for teaching by a severe apprenticeship under schoolmasters of repute. Their aim was to learn all they could, and in such a way as to be prepared at any time to defend their title to the knowledge they had gained.

The real work of the young scholar, who was ambitious to continue his studies, began when he had learned all that was possible from the local schoolmaster. He then left his native place and proceeded to other schools. The undertaking was an arduous one, for the student was poor, he had to travel long distances, he had constantly to prove his aptitude for learning; and his knowledge was repeatedly put to the test. Fortunately, education was held in such high esteem that the hospitality of the peasant and the knowledge of the established schoolmaster were invariably at the service of the humble seeker after learning. The young student was then known as a 'poor scholar,' a figure that looms very large on the romantic side of Irish education at this time. It was possible for him to acquire in this capacity an education to fit him as a teacher; or if he had a vocation for the priesthood to qualify for entrance to an ecclesiastical seminary in Ireland or abroad.

There is a poem in Irish called 'The Poor Scholar's Blessing,'[2] written about the middle of the eighteenth century by a young student who travelled in search of knowledge from Galway to the schools of Kerry. The poem tells of his journey, of the illness that prevented him from reaching his destination, and of the hospitality he received at the hands of strangers:

'Long has been my weary wandering, without one living soul to bear me company,
I have come from the distant North, from far Bananloch,
I have journeyed thence on foot,
I longed to reach the dwellings of the sages, whose houses are in Killarney, by the waters of Lough Lein;
I longed to hear them utter the music of their verses;
I longed to study with them – to be guided by their lore.

'When I left my home in Galway, high hopes surged within my breast;
I reckoned on my talents and on my learning too.
I brought this lore, these talents,
To the highminded, open-hearted sons of the land of Kerry.
But I lost the sweet boon of health.
I made no friends by the way;
I became an outcast from kith and kin.'

There are touching references to the kindness and hos-

pitality shown him. He tells us:
'With tenderest compassion they helped me in my need;
A noble beauteous lady... snatched me from the grave.'
   And again he says:
                                        'Though long I tarried,
None would let me feel the burden of a boon conferred.'
His hostess was a lady of good family, and for those
days comparatively wealthy. He addresses her:
'Gracious and illustrious lady, whom the Son of God
Loveth for bounteous deeds
Thy charity is not in vain.
The priest, the monk, the scholar bless thee!
Thou hast the blessing of the maids
Who seek no earthly spouse.'
   Many of the old Irish families had still a great regard
for the poet and the scholar; but it was usually among
the peasantry that the stranger found the heartiest welcome. 'Blessed with a potatoe to eat,' says a contemporary, 'and a potato to share with a stranger, a poor
Hibernian is happy.'[3] Hospitality was, as M. de Jouy
put it, the 'vertu favorite des Irlandais.'[4]
   Carleton's account of his journey to Munster as a poor
scholar is interesting. He carried with him five pounds
in notes sewn in his coat, and thirty shillings in loose
cash in his pocket. 'My outfit was simple enough,' he
tells us, 'but a portion of it very significant of the object
of my journey. My satchel consisted of a piece of grey-
beard linen, made after a manner of a soldier's knap-
sack, and worn in the same fashion. At a first glance,
every one could see that it was filled principally with
books, whose shapes were quite visible through it, and
the consequence was that my object as a young traveller
was known at a glance. I never stayed in the towns as I
went along, but always at the small roadside inns,
where I was treated with kindness to which I could
scarcely render justice by description.' He points out
how little money he was required to spend on his journey: 'During this youthful pilgrimage such was the

respect held for those who appeared to be anxious to acquire education, that, with one exception alone, I was not permitted to pay a farthing for either bed or board in the roadside houses of entertainment where I stopped.'[5]

Crofton Croker informs us that the poor scholar was usually the most promising pupil of the hedge schoolmaster. He also mentions that friendly relations existed between teacher and scholar, a matter on which Carleton expresses a different opinion. 'The highest class of scholars,' writes Croker, 'is composed of men as full grown, and often as old as the master himself, distinguished by the name of 'poor scholars' or 'strangers'. These strangers are, generally, the sons of reduced farmers and natives of Ulster and Connaught, who having swallowed all the classical information within their immediate reach, range through the bogs of Munster to complete their knowledge of Latin, and to acquire the Greek tongue. The village schoolmaster gains little from this class of students; but the glory of possessing pupils who, when they return to their native province, will spread his fame, appears to him an adequate recompense. Nor is his generosity confined to their education; he also contributes his exertions towards their subsistence, and obtains for them gratuitous lodging in some neighbour's cabin.'[6]

Carleton would appear to suggest that the schoolmaster regarded the teaching of a poor scholar as a profitless undertaking. In this view he stands, I think, almost alone.

It seems to have been customary for a schoolmaster to give a favourite pupil a letter of recommendation when the latter was leaving to pursue his studies in another district. Such a letter was called a 'Pass,' which, according to Professor Power, was 'a sort of introductory letter or recommendation given by a poet or teacher to a successful pupil, friend, or protégé; it was sometimes in Rhyme, but more frequently in a peculiar style of stilted and grandiloquent prose, reminding one of the discourse of a public orator on the conferring of honorary degrees.' The 'Pass' given to Richard Fitzgerald by Donnchadh Ruadh MacNamara in 1759 is probably a typical example. The poet, however, makes use of it to express his scorn or his dislike of certain contemporary schoolmasters. The 'Pass' begins by setting forth at great length the physical and mental attributes of the bearer; it demands for him the best of board and hospitality, with full liberty to go where he should choose; and it gives explicit directions that he be allowed to mix only with the learned and refined. 'I ordain and command that he be not forced to associate or eat with illiterates or cowherds, dog-boys, dog-fanciers or cold-whistling fellows, with long, chilly, tiresome and talkative schoolmasters without culture, courtesy, or learning, such as... (here follow the names of some of these schoolmasters, among whom are mentioned 'Giddyhead O'Hackett,' 'Coxcomb O'Boland,' and 'Buffoon O'Mulcahy')... as these have not been initiated or exercised in the elements of beauties of learning or real knowledge: but are continually spoiling and extinguishing the young folks who are without Latin or good manners.'[7]

Croker furnishes a brief and all too general account of the poor scholar's method of acquiring knowledge: 'The enterprising spirit of these literary adventurers is surprizing; they will start from the home of their infancy – traverse the southern parts of the island – visit every village – sojourn in every school – examine every local curiosity, and return to their birth-place, after perhaps a year's absence, without having, for that space of time expended or even possessed a single half-crown; so warm is the hospitality of the peasantry, and so high their respect for learning! With the schoolmaster, too, it is a matter of special pride to be visited from remote distances; and it is not unusual to hear the respectability of a school estimated by the number of its 'stranger pupils.' It is stated by Croker that poor scholars were usually aspirants for the priesthood; 'after wandering in search of learning through the country, they made their way to France, Spain, or Portugal; studied, and were ordained in the colleges of these countries, and returned to exercise their profession in Ireland.' Carleton says that when it was the ambition of a poor scholar to become a schoolmaster the period of study in the Hedge Schools was considerably extended. It was of a different nature too; the scholar aimed at the acquisition of knowledge for a specific purpose, the schoolmaster's ambition was usually literary supremacy. For this reason literary controversies between teacher and pupil became an important feature in the intellectual formation of the schoolmaster.

Carleton states that when a scholar had learned all that his local teacher had to give, he issued a challenge to the teacher to meet him in a contest of knowledge before competent judges. If defeated, the pupil remained under his old teacher; but if victorious, he went on to another school where he continued his studies. Again a contest took place with his new teacher; and once again if victorious he moved on. In this way he increased his stock of general information, acquired real knowledge and became more subtle in argument. After a year or two he returned home, and again challenged his first teacher. If the contest was decided in his favour, he sometimes took over the school while the teacher was compelled to go elsewhere. The position of the hedge schoolmaster was evidently no sinecure; he was liable at any time to be deposed by a younger and abler teacher.

If one may judge by the absence of reference to these contests, they were not common. Carleton, however, would seem to suggest the contrary, for he informs us that he witnessed one at which the local parish priest was the presiding judge. They were bound to become farcical, and it is probable that other means were adopted to establish the supremacy of the more learned schoolmaster.. There is this much to be said in their favour, however: they helped to promote a high standard of knowledge among teachers, and they rendered continuance of studies and efficiency in teaching vital necessities. It would scarcely be wise to rely too much on Carleton's evidence, or to advance the claim that teachers were generally trained in this way. More likely the system, if it did continue to obtain, was considerably modified.

Poor scholars went their rounds in search of knowledge until about the middle of the nineteenth century, long after the introduction of the system of National Education; in fact almost until the last of the old Hedge Schools had vanished. Lady Chatterton, who visited Ireland in 1838, met some poor scholars during her stay: she described them as 'that interesting race who feed their minds with the crumbs of learning that fall from the hedge schools, and their bodies with the stray potatoes they pick up in the farm-houses.'8

The professional status of the schoolmaster was usually determined by his reputation for knowledge and his success as a teacher. Hence his aim was immediately to achieve a name for wit and learning, and afterwards increase his local reputation by the success of his teaching. Though the co-operation of the people whose children he taught was indispensable to him at the outset, it rested with the schoolmaster when once established to keep up the attendance at his school. The Hedge Schools, it will be remembered, were under the direct authority of their teachers, generally owned by them and always depending for their existence upon the fees paid by their pupils. On the entrance of a rival into the field, it behoved the schoolmaster to defend his ground successfully, or move to another district. When two teachers settled in the same neighbourhood the rivalry between them often became very acute. We are told that when Peter O'Doirnín and Maurice Gorman both taught schools at Forkhill, County Armagh, the latter lost all his pupils and was forced to leave the district because of a satire written upon him by O'Doirnín. This method of displaying one's own powers by showing up a rival's weaknesses dates back to the Bardic Schools. The rivals here were, both of them, scholars and poets.

The hedge schoolmaster was not wanting in diplomacy. Necessity compelled him to be something of a showman. Peter Daly's letter to his friends at Bohermeen is evidence of this. He makes a shrewd reference to some of his rivals who were suspected of taking assistance from one of the 'Bible Societies':

'In teaching the young our old *Mother Tongue*
At least I may venture to mention,
I'm better than some who greedily thumb
The Bible-Society-Pension.'

A more daring method of propaganda was adopted among town teachers who used the newspaper as their medium of self-advertisement. Beneath two notices in 'Finn's Leinster Journal,' dated Jan 2. 1793, announcing the results of the Christmas examinations in Mr. Lawler's School, and in Mr. Buchanan's English Academy, Coalmarket, Kilkenny, there appears the following:

'CARRICK-ON-SUIR SCHOOL.'

'Vacation will commence on the 21st instant, and end on the 20th January.

'Mr. O'Brien requests that the Gentlemen who honour him with the Education of their Children, may be so obliging as to get them examined during the Vacation, which mode will, perhaps, better ascertain their Proficiency than those examinations at School which may be conducted with Partiality and even Deception. An excellent Mathematician *lives in the House,* who instructs the young Gentlemen in Writing, Arithmetic, Book-keeping, and the Branches requisite for Those who may be intended for the Revenue, the Army, the Navy, or the University.   December 20, 1793.'

The tone of this certainly indicates professional jealousy but, none the less, it points out the teacher's readiness to submit his pupils to external and independent examination. It suggests a weakness or laxity in the method of examination, which would imply a corresponding inexactness in the results. In good country schools where the business of education was of paramount importance to both teachers and pupils, much less attention was given to examination and more to the actual progress of individual scholars.

Schoolmasters did not achieve local fame only; their reputation among the body of teachers and among the people generally was almost national. Pupils came to them from all parts of the country either as paying students, or as poor scholars; and after two, three or four years' arduous work they returned to their native places to prove as schoolmasters themselves, the merits of their teachers, or they went to the Continent to continue their studies – and to remember for a long time the comparative greatness of their earlier tutors' scholarship.

Thus, within the body of hedge schoolmasters, and entirely controlled by them were all the factors essential for promoting a knowledge of the elements of the content of education, opportunities of cultivating a taste for languages, literature and mathematics, and means by which even the poorest scholar might receive advanced instruction. There were numerous points of contact between teacher and taught; and between parent, teacher and pupil; all contributing to a healthy activity in education, and playing an important part in the making of the hedge schoolmaster.

NOTES

1. Mason: Parochial Survey. Vol. I. p. 329.
2. Printed in O'Connell: Last Colonel of the Irish Brigade Vol. I. pp. 57–60. (English version only).

3. Hibernian Society. 12th Report. p. 23.
4. L'Hermite en Irlande. Vol. I. p. 133.
5. Autobiography. pp. 69–70.
6. Researches. p. 326.
7. Power: Life of Donnachadh. pp. 11–12; Gaelic Journal. Vol. II. p. 270.
8. Rambles in Ireland. p. 21.

CHAPTER X

The Income of the Schoolmaster

The income derived from teaching was usually very small. The fee paid for spelling was about 1s. 8d. a quarter – in some schools as much as 2s. 2d. was charged. For reading the fee was a little higher, generally 2s. a quarter, while the charge for writing varied from 2s. 2d. to 3s. 3d. a quarter. Arithmetic stood at a higher figure, 4s. 4d. to 7s. a quarter. Latin was about 11s.; 'the schoolmaster at Ennistymon teaches Latin at 11s. 4½d. per quarter.'[1]

At first glance it might appear that the salary thus secured to the teacher was for those days a comparatively good one but it depended on three variables: the number of pupils in the school, their attendance through the winter months and the actual payment of fees.

Since, needless to say, the question of remuneration was an important factor in the schoolmaster's decision to set up an establishment, the number of children at the Hedge School was fairly large as a rule. Though the average number in attendance at the Pay Schools was no more than forty-three, many of these schools had upwards of one hundred pupils. It was evidently not an uncommon thing for the teacher to test the possibilities of a neighbourhood before finally settling down there. Carleton relates that Pat Frayne kept school for only one day in Towney: 'It was his first day of opening the school and also his last in Towney.' He had but three pupils. Later, however, he settled in Skelgy, where he had over one hundred children, boys and girls, in his school. With that number in regular attendance a schoolmaster might reasonably expect a moderately generous return for his labours. Taking it that the majority of children learned reading, a smaller number writing and arithmetic, the teacher's salary might be reckoned at about £50 a year. In actual fact the income of the teacher was usually much less. Even in towns, payment for teaching was poor; in the city of Kilkenny, Frances Grace with a school of 65 pupils had an income of £50 a year, while John Kelly, who taught as many as 117 children made only £40 a year; some town teachers earned little more than £20 a year. Often the meagreness of the salary was due to the poverty or the indifference of the parents. Thomás Ruadh O'Sullivan tells us in one of his poems that he taught for as little as sixpence a quarter:

'It was my shame
To be teaching children for sixpence a quarter.'

Peter Galleghan's income was exceedingly small; the amount he got in fees from his pupils was £6 per annum; at least, that is what is given in the Parochial Returns made in 1824.

Generally speaking, the position in country districts was not so bad, as the teachers were often part paid in kind; turf, butter, eggs, and home-cured meat were to be obtained where money was not forthcoming. 'Every winter's day,' says Carleton, writing of Pat Frayne's school, 'each (scholar) brought two sods of turf for the fire.' He further declares that Pat Frayne 'continued to get more butter from his pupils than five families like his could consume.' Very often, too, the schoolmaster was boarded and lodged free at the houses of the better-off families. Tomás Ruadh O'Sullivan lived in this way for many years. In reference to the school fees usually charged, a contemporary writer observes: 'These have been the terms for half a century back; and the wretched men who are employed in the important business of education, have no encouragement whatever, except the hospitality of the parents of their pupils.'[2]

Attendance at school during the winter was very irregular. This was due to many causes: bad weather, the fact that numbers of children had long distances to travel – when Carleton lived at Springtown, he had to walk a distance of eight miles to school and back – and the unhealthy condition of the schoolhouse itself which was often cold and damp. Consequently fees fell at this time, since those who did not attend did not pay. Sometimes the teacher received in addition to his board and lodging a little money for teaching the children of his benefactor; but as a rule, in poorer districts especially, he was satisfied with his lot if he could tide over the lean period of winter without absolute discomfort.

Occasionally it was difficult to collect the small sums of money owing to the teacher. Such was the case, we learn with the teachers of the Hedge Schools at Kilmactigue, County Sligo: 'Many of these poor schoolmasters,' writes the Rev. James Neligan, an Anglican clergyman, 'do not earn sixpence per day by their continual labours, from the small allowance paid to them, and in many cases promised, but not paid; so that they are often obliged to have recourse to the magistrate, to recover the miserable wages of 1s. 8d. per quarter.'[3] That there were such cases is likely enough, but it is doubtful if the teacher appealed to the law. He had a mightier weapon, which he used with discrimination but without mercy. His power of satire was his greatest asset; and in pillorying his enemies he was careful not to offend his friends.

In one of Peter Galleghan's manuscripts, we come upon some verse evidently written by a schoolmaster who had endured much at the hands of parents.

Thus with school charges so small, the loss of his pupils during the winter months, and the non-payment of fees, the hedge schoolmaster's income was indeed a small one.

The economic position of the teacher was not, however, really so critical. His knowledge and his very status constituted him the leading authority on all matters of moment to the community. His advice and help were sought and generally paid for in money or in kind, and where neither of these were forthcoming he invariably managed to gain in prestige. His social standing in the parish was of considerable importance to him; for the higher it was, the more the people looked to him as guide and counsellor. 'A hedge schoolmaster' writes Carleton, 'was the general scribe of the parish, to whom all who wanted letters or petitions written, uniformly applied – and these were glorious opportunities for the pompous display of pedantry.'[4]

There was a more dignified use than that of mere letter-writing to which the schoolmaster could put his pen. Printed books in Ireland were scarce at this period, and such as were on the market were mostly Bibles, Catechism and Irish Grammars. Irish literature, ancient and modern, was to be found only in manuscript form; rare manuscripts, originals and copies, were scattered throughout the country; poems, songs and stories, many of which had never been written down were on the lips of the people. Here the schoolmaster whose knowledge of Irish was sufficient found employment and exercise for his talents. For his own pleasure he frequently transcribed old manuscripts; more often, perhaps, he was engaged to do so. The work was tedious and difficult, and since many of the manuscripts were in bad condition, it was a test of patience and of skill. A large proportion, I am told, of the Irish manuscripts in the Royal Irish Academy, the British Museum and elsewhere is the work of hedge schoolmasters.

In the Catalogue of Irish Manuscripts in the British Museum there are numerous references to schoolmasters who filled from time to time the important *rôle* of scribe. Thus we find that a certain manuscript was 'written in 1767 by Sean O Cinnéide-i.e.' 'John Kennedy,' who was (says O'Curry, an excellent authority) a schoolmaster at Ballyket, near Kilrush, in Clare.' Another manuscript was 'for the most part written, hastily and in a very poor hand, by a country schoolmaster, that was very well known in his day... at various places in his native county of Limerick and in Clare.' Maurice O'Gorman, who is described as a 'country schoolmaster,' was employed in 1783 by Chevalier O'Gorman to copy out the Dublin Annals of Innisfallen. Michael O'Lonagan, scholar and transcriber of MSS., was also a schoolmaster.

No post brought the schoolmaster into greater prominence than that of parish clerk. It was a position of trust to which no salary wat attached. His added sense of dignity, his friendship with the parish priest, his new and perhaps more intimate relations with the people were sufficient recompense. We can cite Carleton again as an authority: 'The schoolmaster had also generally the clerkship of the parish; an office, however, which in the country parts of Ireland is without any kind of salary, beyond what results from the patronage of the priest, a matter of serious moment to a teacher, who, should he incur his Reverence's displeasure, would be immediately driven out of the parish. The master, therefore, was always tyrannical and insolent to the people, in proportion as he stood high in the estimation of the priest.' Sometimes the schoolmaster was not so easily got rid of. Donnchadh Ruadh MacNamara continued to teach at Slieve Gua long after he had lampooned Father John Casey, of Stradbally; but he had the temerity to do the same to 'a young woman of the parish who promptly retaliated by burning the school house over his head, and forcing him to fly the locality.' In the absence of grave moral faults, the urgent demand for schoolmasters probably assured them their positions. The arrogance which Carleton imputes to them is possibly an exaggeration; it may be no more than a caustic reference to their innocent pride and vanity. Carleton is too fond of the language of hyperbole to be taken very seriously, in this matter at any rate, for schoolmasters were not likely to be offensive to their patrons.

In his Survey of Clare, Dutton states that 'sometimes a trifling addition is made to the master's little income

86

by drawing examinations, bail-bonds, petitions, summonses, etc., etc.' It would almost seem as if the ability to carry out legal transactions was a necessary qualification for the post of schoolmaster, for we find Owen Roe O'Sullivan recommending himself to the people of Knocknagree on the strength of his competence to deal with such important matters as:

'Bills, bonds and information,
Summons, warrants, supersedes,
Judgment tickets good,
Leases, receipts in full,
And releases, short accounts,
With rhyme and reason,
And sweet love letters for the ladies.'

The diary for the year 1793 of John Fitzgerald, a schoolmaster in the city of Cork, is full of references to the various offices he performed for his neighbours, for which there seems to have been recognised charges. Here are a few extracts:

'7th Jan. – Constant smart rain the whole day and most part of the night. Drew marriage articles between Thos. Wood and Bridget Murphy, and got 8s. 1½d. for my trouble. The remainder of the 58th Regt. marched this morning for– – –. Crouch gave me two pots of porter at my fireside. I wrote a letter for him to J. D. Maindue, M.D., Esq., Bloomsbury Square, London.'

'18th April. – A cold, dry windy day. Ed Parks was appointed City Goaler in the place of Thos. Sharp... Wrote a petition for the journeymen horseshoers to raise their wages, and got 2s. 8½d. for my trouble.'

'24th May. – Such another fine day as yesterday. The Union were out this day. I treated Charles Hart to five pots of porter, and he bestowed on me a half hundred of dutchified quills, one quire of large, and three quires of short, letter paper. Wrote a petition for Henry Nicholls, and got 2s. 8½d. for my trouble.'

'29th June – Cloudy, cool weather. Captain Brick sent for me to go to Evergreen, I suppose to draw his Will, but when I went to his house he adjourned the business till to-morrow morning. After I came home Miss Wrixon sent me a posey and some salad. Wrote a petition for Barth. Mahony, and got 2s. 8½d. for my trouble.'

'29th August. – A fine pleasant day; very heavy rain most part of the evening. Began to teach Whetham's son and Parker Dunscombe at Mr. Hinck's school, and is to give me but a guinea a quarter in the future, but I don't know how it will be with regard to the quarter now going on. Cornelius Sweeney gave me 11s. 4½d., and I drew three presentments for him on the new account. Sam Hobbs forced me against my will to drink a tumbler of red wine in his house. I taught Henry Fortescue at Mr. Maguire's house this day, and I drew three presentments for John Raymond, but he gave me no money for them. I drew a fourth presentment for Cornelius Sweeney on the new account, which remains yet unpaid.'[6]

It is probable that the country schoolmaster was quite as actively engaged; though he derived perhaps more prestige than emolument from such duties.

NOTES

1. Mason: Parochial Survey. Vol. I. p. 495.
2. Mason: Parochial Survey. Vol. I. 508.
3. Ibid. Vol. II. p. 374.
4. Traits and Stories. Vol. II. p. 222.
6. These extracts may be found, among others, in the Cork Hist. and Arch. Sos. Journal. Vols. XXIV, XXV, XXXI.

CHAPTER XI

The Social Prestige of the Schoolmaster

The teachers of the Hedge Schools were, with very few exceptions, all men. There is mention of a Dame's school at Piltown, County Kilkenny, but it is specifically stated that it was a school 'for the very young children.' Glassford, who was a member of the Commission of Inquiry into the State of Education in Ireland in 1824, declares that the Hedge Schools would be called 'dames' schools in England.[1] But this is untrue, since in the first place the Hedge Schools were taught by men; and secondly the curriculum was wider, and the standard of attainment was much higher. Dame schools were attended by children up to about the age of seven, and were often merely 'baby-minding institutions' providing at most the barest rudiments of instruction.[2] 'Their educational importance was slight,' whereas the Hedge Schools occupy a worthy position in the history of Irish education. Hence the Irish schoolmaster was immediately on a higher footing than the teacher of the 'dames schools for very young children'; his knowledge was superior, his work was more extensive in scope, he was a teacher of older pupils as well as of younger.

His social standing among the people whose children he taught was remarkably high. He was one of themselves, but different in the respect that he was a man of some learning. They regarded him as a friend whose counsel was to be sought in all circumstances of stress and difficulty, and whose decisions in important matters carried weight. No function of consequence, wedding, christening, or harvest-home took place at which he was not a prominent figure.

A writer of pronounced anti-Irish views gives us a striking sketch of the village schoolmaster of 1820: 'The country schoolmaster is independent of all system and control; he is himself one of the people, imbued with the same prejudices, influenced by the same feelings, subject to the same habits; to his little store of learning he generally adds some traditionary tales of his country, of a character to keep alive discontent. He is the scribe, as well as the chronicler and the pedagogue of his little circle; he writes their letters, and derives from this no small degree of influence and profit, but he has open to him another source of deeper interest and greater emolument, which he seldom has virtue enough to leave unexplored. He is the centre of the mystery of rustic iniquity, the cheap attorney of the neighbourhood, and, furnished with his little book of precedents, the fabricator of false leases and surreptitious deeds and conveyances. Possessed of important secrets and of useful acquirements, he is courted and caressed; a cordial reception and the usual allowance of whiskey greets his approach, and he completes his character by adding inebriety to his other accomplishments. Such is frequently the rural schoolmaster, a personage whom poetry would adorn with primeval innocence and all the flowers of her garland! So true it is that ignorance is not simplicity, nor rudeness honesty.'[3]

Here we have an unintentional tribute to the social prestige of the hedge schoolmaster, and to the democratic spirit of the education with which he was identified. Being himself one of the people the schoolmaster naturally shared their opinions on questions of politics. It was really no discredit to him to recall 'traditionary tales of his country' even of a kind 'to keep alive discontent.' They were probably such tales as would be cherished in any country. This writer is not the only one to charge the hedge schoolmaster with being the organiser of secret political societies, 'the centre of the mystery of rustic iniquity' Carleton does it; the schoolmaster in his sketch, 'The Hedge School,' was a notorious character in this respect. But such writers are very apt to attribute the very worst motives to popular political activities.

The amount of legal business which the schoolmaster was able to transact was immense. He made out wills, drew up leases, measured land, conveyed property; did everything in fact that would ordinarily come the way of a country lawyer. Nearly every schoolmaster possessed copies of the true legal forms of wills, leases, etc., examples of which may be seen in some of the MSS. of Peter Galleghan, who was himself the possessor of many 'useful acquirements.'

The accusation that the schoolmaster was fond of strong drink is scarcely more true of the teaching profession that it is of any other occupation at this time. Indeed surprisingly few references to drinking among schoolmasters are met with, and even these often come under suspicion. For instance, we find a clergyman objecting to the manner of the election of a teacher to an endowed Protestant school at Ballintoy, County Antrim, which, according to the terms of the bequest had to be made by the parishioners assembled at the Easter vestry: 'The only qualification,' he writes, 'necessary, on these occasions, for the candidate to possess is, the capability of drinking whiskey, and sharing it with the electors; and whoever entertains best, and drinks deepest, is sure of gaining his election.'[4] There is no definite reason why the schoolmaster should be specially pointed to as one whose character is complete only when he has added 'inebriety to his other accomplishments.'

Contemporary opinions of the hedge schoolmaster are interesting, even if they are usually adverse. Sir John Carr who travelled in Ireland in 1805 stated that the country schoolmaster was a 'miserable breadless being,' nearly as ignorant as his own scholars. Wakefield is even more critical. 'The common schoolmaster,' he wrote, 'is generally a man who was originally intended for the priesthood: but whose morals had been too bad, or his habitual idleness so deeply rooted, as to prevent his improving himself for that office. To persons of this kind is the education of the poor entirely instructed; and the consequence is, that their pupils inbibe from them enmity to England, hatred to the Government, and superstitious veneration for old and absurd customs.' The Rev. Robert Shaw, writing in 1819, proposed getting rid of the teachers of the Hedge Schools: 'It would be the wisdom of the government and the public,' he said, 'to take it (education) out of the hands of persons ill-qualified to give it a proper direction, and to carry it on under some plan calculated to instil into children principles of moral and civil order, through proper masters and proper books.' Carleton went so far as to state that 'disloyal principles were industriously insinuated' into the minds of the children 'by their teachers.' Yet the schoolmasters might have taught nothing more than a few facts of history that did not reflect credit on a government which for centuries had repressed Ireland (to use the expression of the late Sir Graham Balfour) 'without mercy and without intelligence.'[5]

National history cannot be read without forming prejudices of some kind; and this is more true of a subject race which can only find in its history an account of its past glory, its wrongs and its present plight. No one has yet discovered a conquered race that is entire in its loyalty to its conqueror. Minor illegalities among a free people are merely punishable by law; but when committed by a subject people, they are regarded as open defiance and disloyalty. This point of view must not be overlooked when forming a judgment of the character and political outlook of the Irish Schoolmaster.

Crofton Croker gives an interesting comment on the schoolmaster's standing in the community: 'In Munster,' he writes, 'the village schoolmaster forms a peculiar character; and, next to the lord of the manor, the parson, and the priest, he is the most important personage in the parish. His 'academic grove' is a long thatched house, generally the largest in the place; surrendered, when necessary, for the waking of a dead body, or the celebration of mass while the chapel is undergoing repairs; and on Sundays, when not otherwise engaged, it is used as a jig or dancing house.'

He draws a lively picture of the schoolmaster among his friends: 'In an evening assembly of village statesmen he holds the most distinguished place, from his historical information, pompous eloquence, and classical erudition. His principles verge very closely indeed on the broadest republicanism; he delivers warm descriptions of the Grecian and Roman commonwealths; the ardent spirit of freedom and general equality of rights in former days – and then comes down to his own country, which is always the ultimate political subject of discussion. He praises the Milesian – he curses 'the betrayer Dermod' – abuses 'the Saxon strangers' – lauds Brien Boru – utters one sweeping invective against the Danes, Henry VIII, Elizabeth, Cromwell 'the Bloody,' William 'of the Boyne, and Anne; he denies the legality of the criminal code; deprecates and disclaims the Union; dwells with enthusiasm on the memories of Curran, Grattan, 'Lord Edward,' and young Emmet; insists on Catholic Emancipation; attacks the Peelers, horse and foot; protests against tithes, and threatens a separation of the United Kingdoms! These are his principles, which he pronounces with a freedom, proportioned to the patriotic feeling of his auditory; before congenial spirits he talks downright treason; in the presence of a yeomanry sergeant, an excise officer, a parson's clerk, he reasons on legitimate liberty; he is an enemy to royalty and English domination. Nor do these political sentiments confine themselves to the limits of mere declamation; he is frequently the promoter of insurrectional tumults; he plans the nocturnal operations of the disaffected; writes their threatening proclamations studiously mis-spelled and pompously signed, Captain Moonlight, Lieutenant Firebrand, Major Hasher, Colonel Dreadnought; and General Rock, Night Errant, and Grand Commander of the Order of the Shamrock Election.'[6]

The charge of being implicated in 'insurrectional tumults' can neither be substantiated nor completely disproved for want of evidence. It is probably an exaggeration. We do know that Tomás Ruadh O'Sullivan was a great admirer of O'Connell, the originator of one of the greatest constitutional movements in history; and that James Nash, the Waterford hedge schoolmaster, disapproved of Thomas Francis Meagher's idea of employing physical force as an instrument in Irish politics. Nash, the poor schoolmaster, was a believer in constitutional methods; Meagher, the son of a wealthy merchant, and educated in England, raised the standard of armed revolt in 1847. This is how Meagher, describes Nash: 'The schoolmaster was full of humour, full of poetry, full of gentleness and goodness; he was a patriot from the heart, and an orator by nature. Uncultivated, luxuriant, wild, his imagination produced in profusion, the strangest metaphors, running riot in tropes, allegories, analogies and visions. Of ancient history and books of ancient fable he had read much, but digested little. He was a Shiel in the rough. Less pretentious than Phillips, he was equally fruitful in imagery and diction, and more condensed in expression.'

The gifts of the hedge schoolmaster and his influence were often used on behalf of popular candidates seeking election to parliament, a fact which may account for their unpopularity with the opposing party. This was an honour rarely paid to schoolmasters in other countries. Here is an extract from one of Nash's political speeches, a mixture of audacity, humour and pedantry; he defies the enemies of his native land: 'Let them come on, let them come on; let them draw the sword; and then woe to the conquered! – every potato field shall be a Marathon, and every boreen a Thermopylae.'[7]

The description of the teacher in the village schools of France shortly before the revolution offers many points of comparison with that of the Irish hedge schoolmaster:

94

The master was highly thought of; he assisted the priest in giving religious instruction; he enjoyed the complete confidence of the parents of his pupils; he was honoured by all, and he earned a reasonably good income. Further it sometimes happened that a school passed from father to son for three or four generations.[8]

The Irish schoolmaster enjoyed a prestige at least as high as this; but the remuneration for his labours was rarely as good. It was by no means uncommon too for families in Ireland to devote themselves to teaching for several generations. Father and son occasionally taught schools in the same parish. In Slieverue, County Kilkenny, Daniel Sullivan, Senior, conducted a school of eighty pupils, sixty boys and twenty girls while at the same time his son, also Daniel Sullivan, taught a school at Rathpatrick, Gurteen, a distance of about two miles away.[9] Even father and daughter were sometimes found in charge of schools in the same district; the school in the Catholic chapel at Phillipstown was 'in charge of a girl of fifteen, her father being engaged at another in the neighbourhood'; further, 'nine girls in the school were... preparing for *confirmation*.'[10] The Irish schoolmaster also seems to have been responsible for a large share of the teaching of religious doctrine in the Hedge Schools. We have evidence of this from a comparatively early date. In the diary of Dr. Plunket, Catholic bishop of Meath, respecting his visitation of 1780, there are several statements to this effect: 'The parish clerk or schoolmaster may begin the work of catechetical instruction, but it belongs to the pastor alone to carry it on and finish it with success. This truly great business will never appear important enough to young people unless they hear and see the pastor *himself* teach the Christian doctrine every Sunday and holiday at stated hours. To form the tender souls of young people to virtue, by instilling the saving truth and maxims of our holy religion is one of the noblest functions of the priesthood; it would be a pity to surrender it up to the laity. Were we inclined to do so, we cannot without inevitable danger to ourselves; we are to be the responsible persons at the last day: *animam ejus requiram de manu tua.*' This is clear exhortation to the clergy to take the responsibility of teaching religious doctrine, and not to leave it entirely in the hands of the schoolmaster. On the other hand, it is proof that both parent and priest entrusted the children's spiritual welfare to the teacher.

In the official statements of the French authorities on the independent village schools of France under the First Republic, we find a curious parallel to the kind of criticism prevalent among the opponents of the Hedge Schools; criticism which too often bears the imprint of prejudice and misinterpretation to carry any great conviction with it. In Ireland it was alleged that the schoolmaster aroused and kept alive a spirit of hostility to constituted authority in France, the complaint was that the teacher did not submit quietly to the new *régime.*

One of the very few gratuitous compliments to the character of the schoolmaster comes from the pen of a Protestant clergyman, who wrote from Carne, the extreme easterly point of County Wexford: 'There is one school, not endowed, where almost every child, from five years old and upwards, goes for instruction in spelling, reading, writing, and arithmetic, and some are also taught the Latin classics... At this school (the master of which is James Fortune, of the Roman Catholic religion, a man of very correct morals) are to be seen between 70 and 80 children of both sexes in the summer season, all decently clothed.'[12] The entire population of Carne was 640.

The lovable character of certain of the hedge schoolmasters is fortunately portrayed for us by friends and benefactors who knew them intimately. The following note was discovered in a manuscript compilation of Peter Galleghan, which is in the library of Edinburgh

University: 'These 16 volumes of Irish manuscript were willed and given to me by Peter Galleghan, a hedge schoolmaster and good transcriber of Irish manuscripts and collector of Irish songs – in the year 1855. He lived near Kells in the Co. Meath, and was very thankful to me for some little kindness which I conferred on him and on his only relative – a niece since dead – I doubt much if any of our national schoolmasters have the talent, perseverance and patriotic feeling that this poor fellow possessed. I trust that I have to a certain extent rendered him independent and happy in his latter days without his applying to any society for his support (of which he had the greatest abhorrence). He was one of the most single-minded and honourable and upright men that I have ever met, and was I believe the last of that noble class of the last century called 'Irish Hedge Schoolmasters.' He knew nothing of Classics and differed in this from his fellow 'Hedge Schoolmasters' in the South and West – but his heart and feelings even in his lowly position were such as every Irishman may be proud of. He has gone that road which we all must travel, would that all our lives were as blameless as his.' The note is signed 'E.G.F.'; and on the inside of the cover of the MS. opposite the last page is the inscription: *Ex libris Eugenei Guilford Finnerty.*[13]

Thomas Francis Meagher, wealthy, educated, gifted, an eloquent speaker, and a distinguished soldier, pays a fine tribute to the character of James Nash, as he records the death of the old hedge schoolmaster: 'Like all the poor, honest, gifted men – the rude bright chivalry of the towns and fields – who thought infinitely more of their country than of themselves – he died in utter poverty companionless, and nameless.'[14]

Galleghan and Nash were two schoolmasters who continued to teach long after the National System of Education had been established and had made almost next to impossible the existence of independent rural schools; one, the simple country schoolmaster possessing no

great attainments, but industrious and competent to instruct the children of the locality in the rudiments of
knowledge; the other, gifted but eccentric, patriotic but
opposed to extreme measures in politics.

NOTES

1. Tours in Ireland. p. 117.
2. Smith: History of English Elementary Education. pp. 38–9.
3. Thoughts and Suggestions on the Education of the Peasantry
of Ireland. pp. 12–13.
4. Mason: Parochial Survey. Vol. I. p. 158.
5. Educational Systems of Great Britain and Ireland. 2nd Edition. p. 78.
6. Researches. pp. 326–9.
7. Griffith: Meagher. pp. 286–7.
8. Pierre: L'Ecole sous la Révolution Française, p. 18.
9. P.P. 1826–27. XII. pp. 646–7.
10. Glassford: Tours in Ireland. p. 2.
11. Cogan: History of... Meath. Vol. III. p. 39.
12. Mason: Parochial Survey. Vol. III. p. 130.
13. For a copy of this note, I am indebted to the late Professor
O'Toole who examined the manuscript.
14. Griffith: Meagher. p. 289.

CHAPTER XII

The Poet Schoolmasters

Teaching in those days was a profession which seems to have had a particular attraction for those who had a taste for literature. Nearly every Irish poet of the 18th and early 19th centuries appears to have been a schoolmaster; though, needless to say, but few of the great body of schoolmasters were poets. In teaching, the poets had excellent employment for their talents, but not of the kind that brought them any pecuniary reward. It enabled them to exist while they wrote, and gave them, for the practice of their art, a degree of genteel leisure that was unknown to other occupations. The poets may have made unreliable teachers, though it is by no means clear that they did; but their knowledge was invariably above suspicion. Their wit, their eloquence, their views on life, their originality of thought which must have coloured all their dealings with their pupils were more than ample compensation for their failings. They are remembered with sincere affection. Their frailties are forgotten.

The claims of Donnchadh Ruadh MacNamara to notice among the poet-schoolmasters are many: he was a classical scholar, a noted teacher, and an Irish poet of no little merit.

Born in 1715 at Cratloe, County Clare, he disappears from view till 1740. Nothing is known of his early education; though it is generally believed that he was a student at one of the Irish colleges at Rome, but of this there is no definite assurance. Foley[1] appears to think that his education was completed at Limerick. In 1740 he was teaching in Coffey's classical school at Sliabh Gua, near Dungarvan. It may be of interest to mention here that this school prospered under successive teachers for more than eighty years afterwards. MacNamara's stay was not of long duration. He opened a school of his own in the parish of Modeligo, two or three miles away. In 1743, he had again moved; this time to a district known as 'The Barony,' near Youghal. He is supposed to have gone to Newfoundland in 1745; for one of his important poems deals with his voyage there. However, Professor Power dismisses this notion and believes that he spent the ten years following 1745 in the neighbourhood of Waterford city.[2] O'Reilly, writing much nearer to Donnchadh's time, is much of the same opinion.[3] He is next heard of in 1759 teaching at Ardeenlone in the parish of Newcastle, about ten miles from Waterford. He called his school 'At – na – Scoile.' From here he dated his 'Pass' to Richard Fitzgerald, and hither came James Gray, a poor scholar, from the County Meath to be taught by Donnchadh Ruadh.

The Poet seems to have offended the clergy, the people, or his brother poets, for in 1764 he was compelled to give up his school, and another was appointed in his place. About this time he conformed to the Established Church, and was appointed clerk to the Protestant church of Rossmire, near Kilmacthomas. His successor at the school, according to tradition, did not have an easy time; 'Donnchadh dismissed from his school, and smarting under the indignity, and its practical consequences, made formal report – so, at any rate, it is stated – against the teacher appointed in his stead,' and he, too, had to give up the school to escape punishment by the law. This action does not reflect any credit on the poet. It is known, however, that he afterwards repented of what he had done. The later part of his life was passed in the neighbourhood of Kilmacthomas, County Waterford, where he is supposed to have been tutor in various families. He died in 1810, at the great age of ninety-five.

As a schoolmaster Donnchadh seems to have enjoyed a wide reputation. He had an excellent knowledge of Irish; for years after his death, students boasted that they had learned their Irish from him. His knowledge of Latin was considerable. At the age of eighty he wrote an epitaph in Latin for Tadhg Gaedhealach O'Sullivan, a fellow poet, friend of his later years.

In his study of the Munster poets of the 18th century, Professor Corkery gives MacNamara a high place in his list of minor poets. 'One beholds in him,' he writes, 'a many-sided genius, wanting neither in depth nor in wit, nor in music, nor in strength, as reckless of his power, of his only riches, as he was of everything else, temporal and spiritual.' His ode to the hills of Ireland has been rendered into English verse by James Clarence Mangan. The poem treating of his supposed voyage to Newfoundland, 'The Adventures of a luckless Fellow,' is his longest and greatest work. Professor Power describes the poem as 'a kind of burlesque Aeneid in which the poet, in playful mockery, affects to narrate hiw own adventures;' he says that in it 'there are passages of much eloquence and fire, and throughout there is evidence of considerable poetic power.' O'Reilly points out that 'there are some lines by no means inferior to any of Virgil's.'

In this poem Donnchadh Ruadh, as he was popularly called, makes one or two references to his profession:

'Teaching school was my daily work, and to tell you the truth, it isn't a paying job.' And again when he speaks of his friend William Moran:

'I would prefer...
To exchange all that I have here written
Just to be once more at home, or in some sea-port town;
To be in the Barony, growing rich among the Gaels,
Singing my songs and chastising my scholars,
Or with the priest – who gave me good and gentle advice,
And was generous with his ale.
Or on bright Sliabh Gua than which there is no place

more renowned
For entertaining poets, men of learning and scholars,
Or with the high-souled and erudite William Moran,
Who would chant a poem of ancient form over my still
remains.'

Donnchadh sang to the people; he taught their children;
he sharpened his wits upon them. Yet they seem to have
loved him.

A notice of his death appeared in 'The Gentleman's
Magazine,' November, 1810: 'Oct. 6. At Newtown, near
Kilmacthomas, in his 95th year, Denis Macnamara,
commonly known by the name of Ruadh or Redhaired.
During 70 years, at least, of such a rare course of
longevity, this extraordinary man had been looked
up to by his contemporaries in Irish literature, as
possessing that poetical eminence which ranked him
among the most celebrated of the modern bards.'

A far greater poet than Donnchadh Ruadh taught a
little school in the village of Feakle, County Clare in
1770. He was Brian Merriman, the author of 'Cúirt an
Mheádhon Oidhche' (The Midnight Court). Very
little is known of his life: he was born near Ennis in
1747; he was a teacher at Feakle where he farmed about
twenty acres of land at the same time; he gave up his
school to become resident tutor in the families of the
local gentry; later, he taught mathematics in the city
of Limerick; the news of his death appeared in the
'General Advertiser and Limerick Gazette,' dated
July 29, 1805: 'Died – On Saturday morning, in old Clare-
street, after a few hours' illness, Mr. Bryan Merriman,
teacher of Mathematics, etc.'

Somewhere in his early thirties Merriman wrote
'Cúirt an Mheádhon Oidhche,' a remarkable poem of
over 1,200 lines in length. It was his only extensive
work; beyond two other short poems, nothing else of
his has been found; but that has been sufficient to
establish him as a poet of high rank. 'In the history of

modern Gaelic literature,' wrote Foley, who edited the poem, 'two strikingly original figures stand out – Keating and Merriman – and the latter was the more original of the two. Only by those who have pored over much Gaelic literature can the full extent of that originality be appreciated.' Mr. Stephen Gwynn's criticism of Merriman's great poem is in quite another vein: 'the poem is the nearest equivalent for 'Tam O' Shanter' – but not so proper.'

Owen Roe O'Sullivan, the Kerry poet, was a man of many callings. He was schoolmaster, private tutor, spalpeen, vagabond, sailor and soldier; he began and ended by being a schoolmaster. Like Donnchadh Ruadh the fascination of ruling the literary destinies of a village community lured him back to his original calling. He was born at Meentogues, in the County of Kerry in 1748. He went to a classical academy at Faha, where, Dr. Dineen states, 'the course comprised, besides Irish, English, Latin and Greek. In Greek Homer seems to have been a favourite, and in Latin, Virgil, Caesar and Ovid.'[4] At the age of eighteen he opened a school of his own, but owing to some grave indiscretion he was forced to abandon it after a short time. The next ten years were spent as a spalpeen or itinerant farm-labourer in the counties of Limerick and Cork, or as a wandering schoolmaster, just as it pleased his fancy or he found expedient. He visited his native county of Kerry from time to time, and occasionally taught there during those ten years. For a while he did settle down at Donoughmore, County Cork, and ran a school there. At another period he was tutor to a family called Nagle, who lived near Fermoy. This appointment came to him in a curious way. When he was actually a hired labourer on Nagle's farm, a woman, also a servant of the family, desiring someone to write a letter for her to her master, approached Owen who immediately complied with her request. The letter was supposed to have been written in four languages – Irish, English, Latin and Greek;

but this is very doubtful. Mr. Nagle made enquiries about the writer, and afterwards engaged him to teach his children. But this post, also, he left in disgrace. Sometime later he joined the British Navy, and was attached to a ship in the fleet of Rodney. From the navy he went into the army, and was stationed in England till he managed to obtain his discharge. Then he returned to his native county and set up school at Knocknagree. Shortly afterwards he received a violent blow on the head in a quarrel; he neglected his injury; fever ensued and carried him off at the early age of thirty-six.

He was known to his contemporaries as 'Eoghan an Bhéil Bhinn' (Owen of the Sweet Mouth), so beautiful were the songs and poems that he wrote in the Irish tongue. And critics of to-day pay like tribute to his poetic genius.

He has left one document which is of peculiar interest to us inasmuch as it sets out the entire list of qualifications which a hedge schoolmaster was expected to possess, through strangely enough all mention of classics is omitted. This was a letter to Father Fitzgerald requesting him to announce from the altar on Sunday that the writer is coming to teach at Knocknagree; and that he will give instruction in the Catechism, Euclid's Elements, navigation, Trigonometry, English Grammar, the Rule of Three and Cube Root. This is the order in which the subjects are named in the letter, which was written in crude rhyming verse.

The school at Knocknagree did not last long. The poet's restless nature sent him wandering once more. Had he settled down like Quartermaster Thomas Bryne, the hedge schoolmaster who taught Oliver Goldsmith, we might have had many a better story to tell of him, and more of his musical poetry.

In 1785, a year after Owen Roe's untimely death, there was born, also in the kingdom of Kerry, Tomás Ruadh O'Sullivan – no relation of Owen Roe's, as far as I can father, and later most unlike him in everything ex-

cept in so far as he, too, was a poet and a schoolmaster.[5]
Tomás Ruadh was sent to a school at Gortnakilla, and
afterwards to a college in Dublin. The latter was done
through the kindness of Daniel O'Connell, some of whose
triumphs the boy had celebrated in lively verse. He remained in Dublin for three years when a severe illness
interrupted his education. After convalescing at home
for some time, he refused to go back to Dublin. Then he
became a schoolmaster, and taught in many places in
Kerry, at Cahirdaniel, Portmagee, Aughtubrid, Ballin-
skelligs and Waterville. The only change he had from
this mode of life was during the short time he worked as
postman between Cahirciveen and Derrynane.

   Tomás Ruadh appears to have lived at the houses of
the more prosperous people of the district in which he
taught. His company was eagerly sought; he had a
goodly measure of wit, he played the fiddle well, he sang
his own songs, and he recited with feeling his own poetry and the poems and legends that were his heritage.
Everywhere he was received with hospitality, and
everywhere his hosts became his dearest friends. Unlike many of his dual calling he led a blameless life.
He remained a bachelor; he seems to have had one ro-
mance in his life which is the subject of his song – 'Nóirin
Chnuic na Groidhe.' He was kind, tender-hearted, and
full of good humour. He won the friendship of men like
Father Diarmuid O'Sullivan, the scholar and poet, whom
he styles 'the gentle prince,' and of the great O'Connell, who was always ready to extend to him his patronage.

   In his poetry he does not forget that he is a schoolmaster. He relates in a quaint little poem how much his
schoolhouse is in need of repair:

'I have a little school at Dromcaor
Beside a pleasant and wonderful lake;
All the children from round about come hither,
And all too from every townland in the district,

When the rain comes down from the sky upon us,
My heart is torn with sorrow,
And I came to ask my friends
For a little straw to thatch the roof.'

He possessed, for a schoolmaster who changed the
field of his labours so often, a very large collection of
books. It was an accident that inspired the poem which
tells us what books he had, and loved and cherished. At
this time, he was moving to Portmagee, and in crossing
Derrynane harbour the boat was wrecked; all the bags
in which his books were packed went to the bottom,
'great bags filled with books mostly written with the
pen.' He laments the loss of them in a poem entitled:
'Amhrán na Leabhar' – 'The Song of the Books,' in
which he gives a list of the books that were lost. There
are interesting comments upon some of them or upon
their authors, which show how dear they were to their
owner, and how much he felt the loss of them. The poem
finishes with the lines:

'Never again will I send anything
    Upon the sea:
Praise to the King of the bright angels
    Who gave me back my health ,
And saved the crew of the vessel
    From destruction.'

So mild and philosophical an ending, when the sensitive
poet had lost not a mere library, but what he could never
have again – a collection of books which had taken a lifetime to acquire, and a number of manuscripts, the
labour of his own pen! No wonder he cries:

'If I walked through Ireland and Scotland
And France, and Spain and England,
And yet again if I travelled
    In every direction under the moon,

I would not get as many books
That were so full of knowledge and wisdom
Or of such benefit to me.
    Although now they are gone.'

The poet died in 1848. He was sadly missed from many a homely fireside. But his songs lived on, and with them the kindly spirit of the singer.

No one can read the list of books in the possession of Tomás O'Sullivan without wondering how he came by them. They exhibit a remarkable variety, by no means haphazard. Many of them, the histories of Comerford and O'Halloran, for instance, were most expensive books and even Deighan's Arithmetic cost 5s. 5d., Irish; that is five shillings in English coinage. The hedge schoolmaster had little money to spare, sometimes he had scarcely enough to live upon. We can well imagine then the sacrifices he must have made to put a few shillings aside for the purchase of a book. When he could not do that, he had to borrow the book from a more fortunate friend and make a copy of it in his own handwriting – the toil of many arduous hours. But who knows that he did not enjoy every minute of it!

It is not improbable that Tomás O'Sullivan's collection of books represented the typical hedge schoolmaster's library, for a knowledge of many subjects was a practical essential of the hedge schoolmaster's equipment. It secured him a degree of importance in his own profession, as well as in the people's estimation; and it was of considerable value in maintaining the independence of his school. The teacher with many subjects at his command could manage, up to a point, without the help of an assistant. This versatility was often found coupled with an extensive knowledge of one or two subjects showing that while the schoolmaster appreciated the present and material worth of a general knowledge of school subjects, his intellectual activities were not confined within the narrow limits of his immediate work.

The poet schoolmasters were not lacking in academic requirements. Donnchadh Ruadh was well known as a teacher of Irish and Latin; Brian Merriman was described in his obituary notice, not as a poet, but as a 'teacher of Mathematics'; Owen Roe O'Sullivan gives a long catalogue of his own qualifications; and the books of his namesake, Tomás, are admirable witnesses in favour of their owner. The poets probably taught as efficiently as those teachers who had not the gift of song – and with more memorable effect.

NOTES

1. See his Introduction to Eachtra Ghiolla an Amaráin.
2. Donnchadh Ruadh Mac Namara. pp. 6–17.
3. Irish Writers. p. 231.
4. Life of the Poet. p. 40 et seq.
5. See 'The Songs of Tomás Ruadh O'Sullivan'. Collected and by James Fenton. 2nd. Ed.

CHAPTER XIII

The Teacher of the City 'academy'

There was no clear-cut distinction between the town or city 'academy' and the Hedge School proper. They shared the same character of illegality; the curriculum in the 'academy' was practically the same as that of the better class of Hedge School; and many of the town teachers had themselves received their education in the Hedge Schools. What difference there was, was one of opportunities, of environment, and perhaps of results arising from the regular attendance of pupils. Some of the teachers of town schools were remarkable men. But the hedge schoolmasters do not suffer by comparison with the best of them. They had many advantages which he had not; but those who knew and cultivated the Irish language approached so close to the true hedge schoolmaster both in spirit and in tradition that they might be regarded as hedge schoolmasters working under better conditions than their fellow-teachers in country districts.

Gerald Griffin's first teacher, Richard McElligott, presents an interesting study: he was self-taught, pursuing his work with such zeal and industry as to attain a high degree of proficiency in the subjects he set out to teach; his knowledge of the native language and literature was considerable and scholarly; and he wrote an 'exquisite' hand.

In an advertisement in the 'Limerick Gazette' of 1805, we find him describing himself as 'a Teacher of six and thirty years severe Study and uninterrupted Experience, of well-known abilities in every branch of School Education, and of unremitting Exertion in their Improvement.' He was certainly a man of great perseverance and of some originality, and he possessed a large measure of self-confidence. He was author of 'two small works' on Latin and Greek, he informs us, 'the labour of some years, comprizing and applying every principal word, rule, and idiom in both Languages, contrived in such a manner that, it is almost impossible for any student of common understanding not to have a radical, correct, and extensive knowledge of both Languages in half the time usually devoted to these studies.'[1] In another advertisement he gives some idea, a vague one though, of the nature of these works: 'Mc-Elligott will teach, if required, immediately after Lilly's grammar, a small work comprising every elementary word, rule, and peculiarity of the Latin Language; which work in itself is sufficient for a knowledge of the language, for such as may not have leisure to proceed further; and to such as proceed through the Classicks, it will nearly spare them the trouble of consulting a Dictionary throughout the whole course. McElligott begs leave to call the attention of the Public to this small Latin Work, as it and another on the same plan in the Greek Language must, he presumes to say, if Education shall ever constitute a national concern, be considered of the highest rudimental importance.' He seems to have devoted much time to the study of methods of teaching, and, on his own authority to have reduced the labour of instruction and of study to the effective minimum: he 'begs leave to inform the Public, that he teaches to Spell, Read, and Write the English Language correctly; that his rules for Reading, derived from the highest authorities, have never before been fitted for Schools; and that his English Grammar is so clear as to be immediately understood, and so concise as to be easily retained. Penmanship according to the only method that leads to facility and correctness; a Method unknown in our Schools. Arithmetick and Book-keeping on the most concise and elementary principles in less than one-third of the usual time... Geography in a much more clear simple and concise manner than has ever appeared in print...'[2]

Griffin's biographer, the novelist's brother, relates that as an uncouth boy McElligott entered a 'large and respectable school' in Limerick, and declaring that he would not follow his father's trade, earnestly begged for a position as teacher in the school. His only qualification was his handwriting which 'could scarcely be distinguished from an engraving'; and on the strength of this he was appointed 'writing master.' Thus began the career of Richard McElligott. '(He) was soon induced by one of the more advanced scholars to learn the classics to which, as well as to other studies necessary to a teacher, he devoted himself with so much energy, and made such progress, that he soon had the proud satisfaction' of becoming by sheer industry 'a most respected classical teacher in the city.' In this capacity he acquired a reputation as 'a man of singular ability and industry,' and one who saw to it that his pupils did not shirk their work; 'he was a good teacher, and knowing well from his own experience, what it was possible to accomplish by industry and attention, would take no excuse for neglect, but punished those who were guilty of it in such a manner, as gave him a character for great severity.'[3]

He was pedantic, and perhaps a trifle conceited; pardonable faults in one who had achieved so much through his own efforts. Gerald Griffin's brother tells an amusing story of his mother's conversation with him on the subject of her sons' education: 'My mother went to school with the boys on the first day of their entrance; 'Mr. McElligot,' said she, 'you will oblige me very much by paying particular attention to the boys' pronunciation, and making them perfect in their reading.' He looked at her with astonishment. 'Madam,' said he abruptly, 'you had better take your children home, I can have nothing to do with them.' She expressed some surprise. 'Perhaps, Mrs. Griffin,' said he, after a pause, 'you are not aware that there are only three persons in Ireland who know how to read.'

'Three!' said she. 'Yes, madam, there are only three – the Bishop of Killaloe, the Earl of Clare and your humble servant; reading is a natural gift, not an acquirement. If you choose to expect impossibilities, you had better take your children home.' My mother found much difficulty in keeping her countenance, but confessing her ignorance of this important fact, she gave him to understand that she would not look for a degree of perfection so rarely attainable and the matter was made up.'

In the meagre account given by Griffin there is no hint of condescension, no note of patronage; the writer simply pays a direct tribute to the sterling qualities of this gifted, if somewhat eccentric, schoolmaster. McElligott was a contributor to the first volume of the 'Transactions of the Gaelic Society of Dublin,' of which he was an honorary member. His contribution was 'a very able and learned essay... on the grammatical structure and literature of the Irish Language,' running to forty pages, and exhibiting an extensive knowledge of works on Latin, Irish and English grammar. The other two names that appear in this volume are those of the well-known Irish scholars, Theophilus O'Flanagan and Professor O'Brien of Maynooth College. He was also believed to have written an Irish grammar, which does not appear to have been published. Like the dictionaries of O'Connell and Fitzgibbon, and the Irish Grammar of James Scurry, it probably could not be put on the market without some financial assistance. In the long list of subscribers to the second edition of Deighan's Arithmetic, there appears the name of McElligott, where he is described as 'Professor of General Languages and Mathematics.'

Mr. T. M. O'Brien, another of Gerald Griffin's teachers, also from the city of Limerick, offers a striking contrast to McElligott. He was a more finished product; he was effective without any ostentatious display of strength; and he showed no trace of pedantry. Whether he had the great native ability of McElligott, it is impossible to say. Gerald Griffin went to his school in Limerick at the age of eleven. 'Here' writes his biographer, 'he had the high advantage of having as an instructor, one who was passionately devoted to the ancient poets, and showed a highly cultivated taste in their study. In addition to his natural bent, he therefore caught up much of this spirit, and from this, as well as from a good natural capacity, made very rapid progress. He was exceedingly fond of Virgil, Ovid, and Horace, particularly the first, which he read with such an absorbing interest that his lessons lost all the character of a schoolboy's task.' After some time he was withdrawn and sent to the village school at Loughill, which is situated on the Shannon about twenty-eight miles from Limerick. The new teacher was a young man lately up from the 'Kingdom of Kerry,' capable but rather unpolished. Gerald Griffin's work under O'Brien was of value to him then. 'The tastes... which he had acquired in Limerick never left him, and there was always a strong contrast between the elegant, yet simple language, which Mr. O'Brien had taught him to seek for in his translations, and the rough, homely and straightforward methods pursued at the village school.'[4] The comparison is clearly in favour of the town teacher.

There was a fourth teacher whom Griffin mentions. When they first lived at Fairy Lawn they had as tutor the teacher of the school in the neighbouring village of Loughill. 'He could only devote the first part of the day to us,' wrote Griffin, 'and he was so active and punctual in his attendance, that we were usually dressed and seated on the side of the bed for some time before we had sufficient light to go to our lessons... We remained with him until breakfast hour when he went away to his school, but usually returned in the evening to give us lessons in writing and Arithmetic.'[5]

What a pleasing picture Griffin gives us of the Irish schoolmaster as compared with those drawn by some of his contemporaries! Griffin was a man of good social position; his facts were drawn from personal experience; and he had no object in setting out anything but the truth, unlike Carleton who must caricature the schoolmaster to attract the interest of his readers, or Sir John Carr who must uphold the best tradition of the 'Tour of Ireland.' The teacher has suffered much from prejudiced and uninformed biographers.

Philip Fitzgibbon was another town teacher who appears to have occupied a position of importance among schoolmasters of his day. He taught Classics, English Grammar, Geography, the use of the Globes, Bookkeeping, and he is said to have been a good mathematician. He was also a scribe; he wrote Irish verse – at least a poem in praise of the Irish Language, translated by Mangan, is generally attributed to him; and he was the compiler of a dictionary, the manuscript of which was evidently mislaid, for though scholars like Patrick Lynch and James Scurry were aware of its existence they could not lay their hands upon it. The notice given him by Ryan in his 'Biographia Hibernica,' published in 1821, is as follows:

'Philip Fitzgibbon was a native of Ireland, and ranked high in the mathematical world. He is likewise celebrated for 'a bit of a blunder' that he once committed, arising from the following circumstances. He was supposed to possess a more accurate and extensive knowledge of the Irish language than any person living; and his latter years were industriously employed in compiling an English and Irish dictionary, which he left completed, with the exception of the letter S, *and that he appeared to have totally FORGOTTEN*. The dictionary is contained in about four hundred quarto pages, and it is a remarkable instance of patient and indefatigable perseverance, as every word is written in roman or italic character, to imitate printing. This with many other curious manuscripts, all in the Irish language, he bequeathed to his friend, the Rev. Mr. O'Donnell. During what year he was born is not known, but he died at his lodgings in Chapel-lane, Kilkenny, in April, 1792.'

Fitzgibbon died at the age of eighty-one. His dictionary was never printed, and the manuscript has not yet been found.

One of the most distinguished teachers of town schools was one who was himself a product of the Hedge Schools. This was Patrick Lynch, a native of the County Clare, who received his early education from a schoolmaster at Ennistymon. 'His master knew no English,' writes a contemporary, 'and young Lynch learned the classics through the medium of the Irish language... acquiring... an excellent knowledge of Greek, Latin and Hebrew.'6 His studies were interrupted for about five years owing to the necessity of lending a hand on the farm at home. After that he became in turns usher in a school at Cashel, private tutor to a family in County Kilkenny, and teacher of a school at Carrick-on-Suir where, it appears, he supported the widow and children of his predecessor.

In 1808 he was proprietor of the 'Classical and Mercantile School at No. 30 Lower Ormond Quay,' Dublin, and in 1815 he was appointed secretary to the Gaelic Society which was founded for the preservation and translation of Irish manuscripts and the study of the Irish language. He died in 1818 at the age of sixty-four.

Lynch was a writer as well as an unusually good teacher. His first work of real importance was 'The Pentaglot Preceptor: or Elementary Institutes of the English, Latin, Greek, Hebrew, and Irish Languages, Vol. 1., containing a complete Grammar of the English Tongue. For the Use of schools, and peculiarly calculated for the Instruction of such Ladies and Gentlemen, as may wish to learn without the help of a Master.' This was issued at Carrick in 1796. A second edition of this appeared in 1805, under the title of 'A Plain, Easy and Comprehensive Grammar, of the English Tongue; in which the definitions & Rules necessary to be committed to Memory are composed in Familiar Verse, with a

Preliminary Essay, containing, among many other useful Observations on the Theory, Structure and Analogy of Languages in general, A Critical Review of the most celebrated English Grammars hitherto Published.' This also came from the press at Carrick.

He did not get out the remaining volumes of the 'Pentaglot Preceptor,' as he originally intended, but he published in 1817 a little book of 104 pages, entitled: 'The Classical Student's Metrical Mnemonics, containing in Familiar Verse, all the necessary Definitions and Rules of the English, Latin, Greek and Hebrew Languages.' It is evident that Lynch had a number of completed works on hand, for in the same year two other books came out. One was a text-book of elementary astronomy – the title of this is comprehensive and attractive: An Easy Introduction to Practical Astronomy and the Use of the Globes: including, in Mnemonic Verse and Rhyming Couplets, as the most Effectual Means hitherto invented for Assisting the Memory, the necessary Axioms, Definitions and Rules of Chronology, Geometry, Algebra and Trigonometry, with the Prognostics of the Weather, &c., &c. For the Use of Schools and Young Ladies.' The other was a text-book of the geography of the world and a history of Ireland, the title of which reads: 'A Geographical and Statistical Survey of the Terraqueous Globe including a comprehensive Compend of the History, Antiquities and Topography of Ireland. Embellished with a Curious Map of Eire. For the Use of Schools and Adult Persons.' This is a work of about 350 pages, of which 190 are given to geography and the remainder to history.

He published a very useful little grammar of the Irish language in 1815, the scope and limitations of which were clearly indicated in the title: 'Introduction to the Knowledge of the Irish Language as now spoken; containing A Comprehensive Exemplification of the Alphabetic Sounds, and a complete Analysis of the Accidents of the declinable Parts with the pronunciation of each

Irish word employed in Illustration, so far as could be effected by the substitution of English Characters Systematically arranged and Methodically disposed in fourteen short Synoptic Tables.' He also wrote a life of St. Patrick, a work of which John O'Donovan, the famous Irish scholar, had a high opinion, and a life of St. Columcille, both of which were published. He edited Alvary's Latin Prosody and Wettenhall's Greek prosody; and for a time he was responsible for the success of Grant's and Lady's Almanacks. At the time of his death he had several other important works in hand which were never published.[7]

Lynch's writings show a thoroughness, accuracy and finish that could scarcely be expected from one who wrote so much and upon so many subjects and who, while he was writing, was engaged in the laborious occupation of teaching. They are clearly the fruits of industry, patient research, wide reading and, in the case of The Classical Student's Metrical Mnemonics, much ingenuity. How long he spent upon any particular work is not known but it must be observed that most of his important books were not published till he was over sixty, when he had been nearly forty years teaching.

In the list of subscribers to the Pentaglot Preceptor there are the names of teachers, scholars of repute, university professors, Catholic and Protestant clergymen, and distinguished laymen, showing the high opinion in which Lynch was held by his contemporaries. And posterity has not reversed their judgment.

McElligott and Lynch were undoubtedly outstanding figures among the teachers of their day. But they did not overshadow the hedge schoolmaster. If anything, the relative achievements of the latter were greater, and of a more enduring character.

NOTES

1. Possibly in manuscript. I can find no trace of them.

2. Limerick Gazette. January 31 1815.

3. Works of Gerald Griffin. 1843. Vol. I. pp. 16–19.

4. Works of Gerald Griffin. pp. 50, 51.

5. Ibid. p. 42.

6. Warburton: Hist. of Dublin. Vol. II. p. 916. See also O'Casaide's article in Waterford Arch. Soc. Journal. Vol. XV. p. 47 et seq.; and author's article in STUDIES. Sept. 1931.

7. Seumas O'Casaide gives a complete list of Lynch's published and projected works in Waterford Arch. Soc. Journal. Vol. XV. pp. 107–120.

CHAPTER XIV

The Last of the Philomaths

The dictionary of a hedge schoolmaster named Peter
O'Connell, who was born at Carne in the County of
Clare about 1743, forms a landmark in the history of
Irish scholarship. The dictionary was the work almost
of a lifetime; it was begun in 1785, and was completed
only a short time before O'Connell's death some forty
years later. O'Connell received assistance, facilities at
least, for his work, from Charles O'Conor of Belanagare,
and from Dr. O'Reardon of Limerick with whom he
lived from 1812 to 1819. It was never published. The
original manuscript, of which there is a copy in Trinity
College, Dublin, was secured by Hardiman, and sold by
him to the British Museum, although he had promised
O'Curry that he would never let it pass from Ireland.[1]

A memorandum by Hardiman on folio one gives some
of its story: 'The compiler was the best Irish scholar of
later times – He was forty years occupied on this Dictionary, to which he was continually adding to his death,
which happened near Kilrush in the County of Clare abt.
the year 1826 – when he had it complete for publication.
It is the most copious Dictionary ever compiled, and is
particularly valuable for explaining the *ancient* Irish,
and manuscripts of Ireland.

'He was for a long time with old Charles O'Conor at
Belanagare; & was several years in the highlands of
Scotland, where he acquired many ancient words and
phrases.

'When I heard of his death, I was apprehensive that
this work wd. be lost & I went from Dublin to Kilrush where I purchased it from his friends, and had it
transcribed for the press.'

O'Curry, who knew O'Connell well, and was probably
one of his pupils, had a high opinion of the work while

the late Dr. Standish O'Grady considered that O'Curry's estimate was far too low. According to Dr. Kenney, the American scholar, O'Connell, the hedge schoolmaster, was 'one of the most remarkable of the forgotten scholars of the early nineteenth century.'[2]

There was at Callan, County Kilkenny, a schoolmaster named Humphrey O'Sullivan, who was a collector of Irish MSS. Many of his manuscripts are in the library of the Royal Irish Academy, while some few are to be found in the library of Maynooth College. He is also said to have written poetry. But his most interesting contribution to literature is his diary, the singular qualities of which so favourably impressed O'Curry. 'This diary,' the latter wrote, 'contains observations on the state of the weather, Irish botany and ornithology, fairs, markets, politics, history, war, peace, etc., etc. It is a very curious and, indeed, important document on account of the various topographical, historical and botanical observations it contains... There is not, perhaps in existence so minute and circumstantial a record of those years as the present; and the language in which they are expressed is very correct, and sometimes elegant.'[3]

The author was son of Denis O'Sullivan, also a schoolmaster, who had migrated from Kerry to the County Kilkenny about 1790. Both father and son taught in Callan for some years. The father died in 1808. Humphrey, finding later on that teaching was more of a crutch than an actual support, opened a draper's shop in Callan. He continued teaching, though, till 1831.

A more recent testimony to the value of this unusual work is given by Mr. Seamus O'Casaide, who has edited the diary for the year 1827: 'In the history of modern Irish literary effort his diary holds a unique place. No such Irish diary has hitherto been published, and it is more than probable that no other such diary has been preserved. It reveals its author as at once a genuine patriot, a close and affectionate observer of nature and of rural life and a man who though engaged in the routine of business was yet of a poetic and romantic turn of mind.'[4]

No more eloquent tribute could be paid to Humphrey O'Sullivan's diary than the handsome volumes, issued by the Irish Texts Society and edited by the Rev. Michael McGrath, S.J. with a translation that reflects both the charm and the spirit of the original.

Many schoolmasters seem to have had a special pride in bringing something more to their work than what was immediately necessary. The compiled manuscript volumes of interesting and, often, curious information. These manuscripts appear to have been quite common at one time: Crofton Croker, writing in 1824, says that they 'may be met with in almost every village,... To hear the contents of one of these monstrous olios read aloud, is considered by the peasantry a treat of the highest order, and large numbers will assemble on a winter's evening around the turf fire of a farmer's cabin for that purpose.'[5]

Peter Galleghan, as we already know, wrote a good many volumes of this kind. The one that I examined, then the property of the late Professor O'Toole, was entitled: 'Peter Galleghan's Collections in English and Irish, Entirely Written by Himself' and dated 'January 16th 1824'. Its contents, covering 838 quarto pages bound to a strong leather back, consisted of a sort of cyclopaedia of general, useful and, sometimes, valuable material: literature, history, geography, mathematics, astronomy, medicine; everything, indeed, that the needs of a village community would demand, and much that would add to its intellectual store.

When we consider the circumstances in which Peter Galleghan's lot was cast, we cannot but admire the courage, industry and perseverance which must have marked the daily round of his life. He probably wore a threadbare coat, he must have been often without things which we would call necessities, yet he managed to buy good paper on which to write, good pens, good ink, and to find some secluded place in which to write in that elegant, finished hand of this.

The statement of his teaching, given in this volume, during a period stretching over twelve years, 1814 to 1826, tells the story of what must have been the experience of many a hedge schoolmaster; it is an epic of trials and disappointments, and of a seemingly great struggle for existence. The official returns of the Commissioners of the Board of Education in 1825 give the naked facts: Peter Galleghan's school is described as a 'Pay School'; the building in which he taught was 'a stone wall cabin' costing about £5; the number of his pupils was 42; he was unassisted by any Society or by local patronage; and his 'Total Annual Income... arising in all ways from the School' amounted to about £6. From his own record of twelve years' teaching, we learn that the longest continuous period during which he taught in all this time was seventeen months; the shortest was only a couple of weeks – and short periods were not uncommon. There were gaps of three, four, even eight months when he did not teach; and, it must be noted, these periods were not confined to any definite part of the year, showing that it was want of a school-house, rather than the rigours of winter or the abundance of employment in summer, that interrupted his work. However hard the life of a hedge schoolmaster may have been, there was always the knowledge that a warm welcome awaited him whenever he pushed open the half-door of the humblest dwelling.

Life was increasingly difficult for men who endeavoured to maintain the independence of their schools after the establishment of the National Board of Education in 1832. They witnessed the passing of the old Hedge Schools, slowly giving way to the schools under the National Board. Parents were sending their children to them, because the fees were lower than in the Hedge Schools. Teachers in both town and country schools were taking posts in them because there they would be sure of a regular salary, small though it might be. And the

Hedge Schools and other pay-schools, where classics and mathematics were taught, were disappearing because of the dearth of pupils.

The poor scholar and the hedge schoolmaster have not lost their place in the affection of the people, nor even in the literature of our own day. In his poem, 'A Poor Scholar', Padraic Colum describes what may have been the feelings of many a schoolmaster who loved his Latin and Greek, and who saw, or could not fail to see, his day drawing to a close, fading sunless into the darkness of night:

'My eyelids red and heavy are
With bending o'er the smould'ring peat.
I know the Aeneid now by heart,
My Virgil read in cold and heat,
In loneliness and hunger smart.
　And I know Homer, too, I ween,
　As Munster poets know Ossian.

'And I must walk this road that winds
'Twixt bog and bog, while east there lies
A city with its men and books,
With treasures open to the wise,
Heart-words from equals, comrade-looks;
　Down here they have but tale and song
　They talk Repeal the whole night long.

'You teach Greek verbs and Latin nouns,'
The dreamer of young Ireland said.
'You do not hear the muffled call,
The sword being forged, the far-off tread,
Of hosts to meet as Gael and Gall –
　What good to us your wisdom store,
　Your Latin verse, your Grecian Lore?'

'And what to me is Gael or Gall?
Less than the Latin or the Greek.

I teach these by the dim rush-light,
In smoky cabins night and week.
But what avail my teaching slight?
    Years hence, in rustic speech a phrase,
    As in wild earth a Grecian vase!'

NOTES

1. O'Curry: Catalogue of Irish MSS. in the British Museum. 1840. p. 81 et seq.
2. Sources for the Early History of Ireland. Vol. I. p. 67.
3. Hodges and Smith Catalogue (R.I.A.) p. 532. Quoted by Seumas O'Casaide.
4. Gadelica. Vol. I. p. 53 et seq.
5. Researches. pp. 331-2.

INDEX

126

MORE MERCIER BESTSELLERS

LETTERS FROM THE GREAT BLASKET

Eibhlís Ní Shúilleabháin

This selection of *Letters from the Great Blasket,* for the most part written by Eibhlís Ní Shúilleabháin of the island to George Chambers in London, covers a period of over twenty years. Eibhlís married Seán Ó Criomhthain – a son of Tomás Ó Criomhthain, An tOileánach (The Island-man). On her marriage she lived in the same house as the Islandman and nursed him during the last years of his life which are described in the letters. Incidentally, the collection includes what must be an unique specimen of the Islandman's writing in English in the form of a letter expressing his goodwill towards Chambers.

Beginning in 1931 when the island was still a place where one might marry and raise a family (if only for certain exile in America) the letters end in 1951 with the author herself in exile on the mainland and 'the old folk of the island scattering to their graves'. By the time Eibhlís left the Blasket in July 1942 the island school had already closed and the three remaining pupils 'left to run wild with the rabbits'.

MÉINÍ
THE BLASKET NURSE

LESLIE MATSON

This is the life story of a remarkable woman, Méiní Dunlevy. Born in Massachusetts of Kerry parents, Méiní was reared in her grandparents' house in Dunquin. When she was nineteen, she eloped with an island widower to the Great Blasket, where she worked as a nurse and midwife for thirty-six years. Returning widowed to Dunquin, she died in 1967, aged 91.

Méiní's story, recorded by the author from her own accounts and those of her friends and relatives in Dunquin, is an evocation of a forceful, spicy personality and a compelling reconstruction of a way of life that has exercised an enduring fascination for readers. *Méiní, the Blasket Nurse* is a worthy successor to *An t-Oileánach* and *Twenty Years a-Growing*.

THE HEDGE SCHOOLS OF IRELAND